PRAISE FOR
OWN IT. LOVE IT. MAKE IT WORK.

At Orangetheory we say, "Don't just wish for it. Work for it." For all of you who know that this is the truth to success, Carson Tate's *Own It. Love It. Make It Work.* is a must-read. There's nothing I love more than a plan—with real steps to follow, practical tools to apply, and above all else, inspiration and energy to motivate you to reach your next level, and then push beyond it.

Ellen Latham, founder and CEO, Orangetheory

Finding your authentic purpose and true happiness in the work that you do is part of your life's divine journey. Not only is *Own It. Love It. Make It Work.;* full of step-by-step guidance about how to find meaning in your work, it's infused with heart and soul, caring and warmth. It's the best of Carson. You'll want everyone you know to read it.

Sonia Choquette, *New York Times* bestselling author, spiritual teacher, and intuitive mentor

Work has radically changed. What we need now more than ever are engaged and fulfilled employees. Carson Tate's newest contribution to productivity, efficacy, and personal fulfillment in the workforce gives us actionable tools and results-driven stories from her consulting practice. She shows employees how to take ownership of their career, their happiness, and their success.

Jill Olmstead, Chief Human Resources Officer, Lending Tree

If you want a professional career coach, you've found one. Carson Tate is empowering, and her practical advice is invaluable. *Own It. Love It. Make It Work.* will help you elevate your skills and relationships so that you are in the right mindset and position to achieve your goals. This is the type of book you will come back to again and again throughout your career, for inspiration and encouragement.

Regina Wharton, HR Executive, Strategist, and Mentor, Financial Services

In medicine, change is constant. *Own It. Love It. Make It Work.* will equip and empower you to not only navigate change in your job and industry, but also show you how to adapt and evolve, so that you can continue to grow in your career, as well as motivate your team to do the same. Filled with motivating stories, real-world tools, and clear strategies, this is the guide you need for the job you have right now.

Solange Benjamin-Thorpe, MD, Medical Director Pediatric CVICU at Levine Children's Hospital, Atrium Health

Learning is at the heart of what we do. With practical tools and uplifting stories, Carson teaches us how to be recognized and rewarded for our own unique skills, knowledge, and contributions. She shows us how to ensure our talents and passions have a stage from which to shine. Above all else, *Own It. Love It. Make It Work.* outlines how to make our jobs fit our lives, not the other way around.

Ginny Norton, CEO Hatch Early Learning

Own It. Love It. Make It Work. is insightful and full of honest candor that provokes readers to explore their potential by evaluating where they are right now. It is a must-read if you are ready to create your dream job!

Tina Craft, Chief Commercial Officer, Albemarle Corporation

This book is a powerful guide to help motivate you, inspire you, and breathe new life into your work. No matter what role you play in your current organization, there is always another level to reach, a fresh goal to set. Reading Carson's book is like having a personal coach encouraging you to do your best, and be your happiest, always.

Alison Lewis, Chief Administrative Officer, Newmark Knight Frank

In *Own It. Love It. Make It Work.*, Carson expertly shows you how to pick your own palette and design your dream job. She shows you how to be fulfilled at work, and how to reengage with your employer and your team, and it provides insightful techniques to maximize your ability to build trust among your peers. Carson references the great Chinese proverb, "A journey of a thousand miles begins with a single step." Read this book and take that career-enhancing step today!

Bill Huber, Chief Financial Officer, VELUX Group USA Inc.

Carson has a special way of telling a story that draws you in and connects with you on a level that is raw and unfiltered. Once again, she has given me a look into my work life that I had not considered before. When you read *Own It. Love It. Make It Work.*, you will see and experience your work life differently.

Davoud Khorzad, PhD, Director, Operations Excellence, AbbVie Commercial

I've read many leadership books in my 31-year career; few, if any, offer such high-quality and practical approaches to work, life, and overall enjoyment in what you do. *Own It. Love It. Make It Work.* is transformational for any leader who desires to reach new levels of personal success while enjoying the journey that is life.

Mark Reed, Head of School, Charlotte Country Day School

Carson facilitated a class for our team members a few years ago, and she is as charming, empathetic, erudite, and helpful in person as she reads in her latest book, *Own It. Love It. Make It Work.* The book is like a well-seasoned meal: the perfect amount of stories, step-by-step tips, research, and humor. Pour a glass of wine and enjoy!

Suz Hahn, Manager of Learning and Development, Daimler

Own It.
Love It.
Make It Work.

Own It.
Love It.
Make It Work.

How to Make Any Job
Your Dream Job

Carson Tate

New York   Chicago   San Francisco   Athens   London
Madrid   Mexico City   Milan   New Delhi
Singapore   Sydney   Toronto

1 2 3 4 5 6 7 8 9   LCR   25 24 23 22 21 20

ISBN   978-1-260-46979-0
MHID   1-260-46979-4

e-ISBN   978-1-260-46980-6
e-MHID   1-260-46980-8

Library of Congress Cataloging-in-Publication Data

Names: Tate, Carson, author.

Title: Own it. love it. make it work.: how to make any job your dream job / Carson Tate.

Description: New York : McGraw Hill, [2020] | Includes bibliographical references and index.

Identifiers: LCCN 2020023458 | ISBN 9781260469790 (hardback) | ISBN 9781260469806 (ebook)

Subjects: LCSH: Job satisfaction. | Quality of work life. | Employee motivation. | Career development. | Work-life balance.

Classification: LCC HF5549.5.J63 T3338 2020 | DDC 650.1—dc23

LC record available at https://lccn.loc.gov/2020023458

McGraw Hill books are available at special quantity discounts to use as premiums and sales promotions or for use in corporate training programs. To contact a representative, please visit the Contact Us pages at www.mhprofessional.com.

To Andrew and EC

CONTENTS

STEP ONE
—— OWN IT. ——

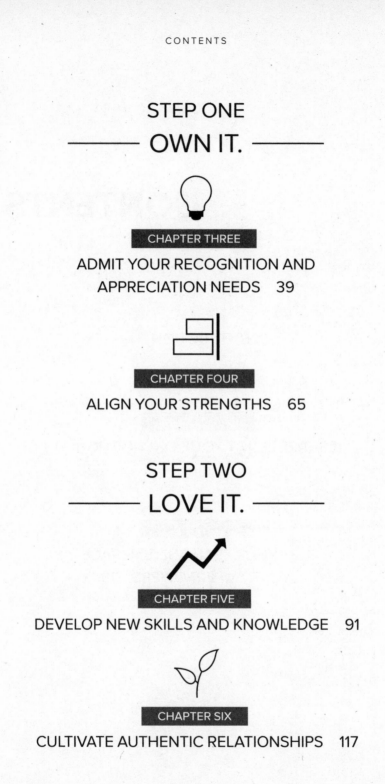

STEP TWO
—— LOVE IT. ——

STEP THREE
—— MAKE IT WORK. ——

YOUR DREAM JOB

ADMIT · ALIGN · DEVELOP · CULTIVATE · DESIGN

YOUR SKILLS + EXPERIENCES + VALUES

STEP ONE:
OWN IT.

ACKNOWLEDGE WHO YOU ARE AND WHAT YOU NEED

ADMIT your recognition and appreciation needs

ALIGN your strengths

STEP TWO:
LOVE IT.

REKINDLE PASSION AND JOY IN YOUR WORK

DEVELOP new skills and knowledge

CULTIVATE authentic relationships

STEP THREE:
MAKE IT WORK.

MAKE YOUR JOB WORK FOR YOU

DESIGN your work to find *your* meaning

INTRODUCTION

Anne's bright, modern office features contemporary art, art deco lighting, and a sleek glass desk with a beautiful white orchid on the corner. As I walked in for our coaching session, I was struck by how she stood out in contrast to her vibrant surroundings. Her mouth pinched tight, her shoulders stooped forward as though she was typing on a computer. As I looked into her eyes, they shocked me—flat, lifeless, absent their usual spark. The look was eerily familiar.

I listened as Anne described her work as a corporate attorney, her service on the local city council, parenting a teenage daughter, and trying to fit in the ever elusive "me" time. Anne had attended one of my webinars on email management and was thrilled that she had implemented most of the strategies. She opened her laptop to show me that there were less than 100 messages in her inbox.

Anne's eyes brightened as she told me she no longer worked 60-hour weeks and had attended her favorite Pilates class twice last week. This week she had incorporated 10 minutes of quiet time into her mornings using the app Headspace. A photo from her family's spring deep-sea fishing vacation completed the picture of a woman who seemingly had it all.

"I imagine you are wondering why you are here," Anne said.

"Yes, I am."

"Well," she said, "I'm using your tools and strategies to help me be more productive and get more done, but something is missing. I am more efficient, but so what? I used to be very goal oriented. I would set goals, and push and strive to achieve them. Each accomplishment became another notch in the armor of my success. Now, when I wake up in the morning, I feel a heaviness in my chest. Not because my work can be challenging or my days too long and full, but there is an emptiness inside. I feel like I am sleepwalking through my days."

Searching for a way to connect to what she needed, I recalled Anne's answer to a question I had emailed her before this session: "What is currently not working well at work?"

She had written: "Getting through all the emails and calls in order to get to the impactful work."

That was it—the impactful work. Anne wanted to achieve something more substantial than simply getting through her workday. She longed to discover how to bring more meaning to her work and how to be more fulfilled and engaged in her work.

I shifted quickly, asking, "What's at stake if you do not get through all the emails and calls and don't get to the impactful work?" Anne paused, thinking for a minute. Then, she said, "A disadvantaged youth in our city won't have choices. He will be limited to a path that leads to a life of unemployment, incarceration, and unrealized potential."

As she uttered these words out loud for what may have been the first time, Anne's eyes welled with tears. Her deeply rooted pain, frustration, and uncertainty flowed down her face. Anne's body intuitively understood that what she desired was much more significant than efficiently and effectively getting work done.

This moment in Anne's office solidified for me what I had been seeing and hearing from more and more of our clients. When they moved beyond frenetic busyness and overwhelm and were more productive, what remained was a desire for *more* from their work and their life. My clients wanted to advance their career, be recognized, and love their work. They wanted their work to have value, meaning, and purpose. They wanted to make a living *and* enjoy their life. And they were not alone.

A disengagement epidemic is consuming the workplace. According to Gallup's 2019 State of the American Workplace report, 65 percent of the United States workforce is disengaged. Just look around your office. Six out of ten of your colleagues are unhappy and dissatisfied and probably experience the "Sunday night scaries," dreading the thought of Monday morning. Too many of us hit snooze on our alarm so many times we lose count because we don't want to get out of bed and go to work. Many of us count down the days until the weekend or our next vacation.

For you and me, the costs of the disengagement epidemic are extraordinarily high. You watch your dreams disintegrate in front of you as you find yourself without the autonomy and support to advance in your career. You realize that what you have been laboring for, striving for while giving up your nights and weekends, lacks purpose and meaning for you. You recognize that your manager's values don't align with your values. It's the self-doubt and slow erosion of your self-worth as you are passed over for a promotion or not selected for that high-profile strategic initiative. You have the devastating thought that this just might be all there is to work and life. You feel—and believe—that you are powerless to change to anything.

In this state, your body suffers. As you experience more workplace stress and have fewer sources of pleasure at work, your body is taxed by high levels of cortisol. You seem to catch whatever is going around the office, and when everyone else is on the mend, you're still filling up your trash can with tissues. You're always tired, and your pants are getting tighter and tighter no matter how many days you go to the gym and avoid the snacks in the breakroom. Your head begins to throb the minute you pull your car into the office parking garage.

Something has to give.

Through our training, consulting, and coaching programs and my first book, *Work Simply*, my team and I have helped hundreds of thousands of people improve their productivity. I was proud of our work. But it was not enough.

Looking back, I now realize that the conversation with Anne was my tipping point. When I returned to my car, something had shifted in me. I could not have one more conversation on the side of the soccer field, in a coaching session, or in the hallway of a client's office where I only sympathized with the anguish of being discouraged and unfulfilled at work. Empathy was no longer enough.

It was time for action. I had a new purpose: find the solution to the disengagement epidemic that consumed the hearts, minds, and souls of the American workforce. And I started where I always start, with research.

To confirm what I'd heard and observed with our clients, and just about everyone I met, I conducted a research survey with more than 1,500 global professionals. More than 53 percent of them stated that their primary goal at this point in their career was being happy at work. But happiness is fleeting. It's an emotion. Happiness is too narrow a yardstick to measure the richness and complexity of your work. What they really want is to be fulfilled at work. The survey respondents told me that they wanted the following:

- "More autonomy in my job to structure my time, where I work, and what I work on."
- "Clarity around the mission, purpose, goals, and big picture of the organization so I can align my skills and know my work matters."
- "More collaboration and relationships at work."
- "To be recognized and rewarded for my knowledge, skills, and contributions at work."
- "The opportunity to develop new skills and knowledge at work. I want to grow in my career."
- "The opportunity to be creative and innovative at work."
- "To receive feedback on my work and the support to achieve my goals."
- "The opportunity to use my knowledge and skills at work."
- "To be compensated for the work that I do."

The pieces of the disengagement epidemic puzzle started to come together. Gratification, purpose, and joy are possible when you can clearly see how your tasks and projects align with and support the organization's mission—a mission for the greater good of our world. It is fostered through meaningful work when you understand how your personal attributes, interests, and values contribute to the work of the organization. Fulfillment is possible when your work is recognized and appreciated for what it is—the full expression of your humanity.

You want to connect with others in a meaningful way and believe that your time and efforts contribute to and positively impact the attainment of the company's goals. You want to know the significance and relevance of your work and to feel that your job contributes to society, a specific community, or a cause. You want to be engaged and fulfilled at work. However, the problem is the current approaches to address and solve the disengagement epidemic are not effective.

For example, one of our clients offers its employees free tickets to sporting events and to our local amusement park, has a beer fridge in the breakroom, and has an unlimited vacation policy. Google, Tito's Vodka, and Mars, Incorporated, all allow team members to bring their dog to work. And let's not overlook the Ping-Pong tables, nap pods, or on-site massages that are provided in numerous offices.

If higher salaries, bonuses, benefits, "perks," or custom-designed office spaces were the antidote to the disengagement epidemic, more than 35 percent of the United States workforce would be engaged. In my work with our clients and in my research, I've identified that the root causes of lack of fulfillment, connection, and purpose at work are much deeper than compensation, benefits, and perks. These are mere surface approaches to a complex, multifaceted, and deeply personal issue.

Your dream job requires much more than a paycheck, free tickets to an amusement park, or a nice office. Perhaps roller coasters make you vomit, you've never liked Ping-Pong, and dogs make you sneeze. These perks are temporary, impersonal Band-Aids. *What's missing from the relationship with your employer is YOU.*

As you know from relationships with family, friends, and significant others, both people in the relationship have expectations of each other, and both of you are responsible for the health and vitality of the relationship. All relationships are based on give-and-take. They are social contracts. The relationship with your employer is no different. However, you probably don't think about your relationship with your employer this way. Your knowledge, skills, and experiences are valuable contributions you *give* to your employer. It takes two to create a vibrant, beneficial, and meaningful relationship. You are a strong and equal partner in your relationship with your employer.

It is time for you to acknowledge and use your power so you can make any job your dream job. You have everything you need inside of you to own, love, and make your job work for you. You just need a map to show you the way. Let this book be your guide.

Own It.
Love It.
Make It Work.

CHAPTER ONE

ESCAPE IS NOT YOUR ONLY OPTION

Warning, going to sleep on Sunday will cause Monday.
Please note that staying awake all night
does not prevent Monday. There is no cure.[1]

I hated my job. I spent all day on the phone making cold sales calls. People hung up on me. People screamed at me. I was called a variety of unpleasant, unkind names. Throughout the workday, my boss, George, would stand behind me in my small, windowless gray cubicle and read my emails or listen to me as I made sales calls. George made insensitive and inept Michael Scott from *The Office* look like an effective manager.

One Thursday afternoon I didn't feel well and left the office at 4:00 p.m. At 4:30 p.m., our home telephone rang.

My husband, Andrew, answered. "Hello?"

"Hi, this is George Smith. Is Carson there?"

"Yes, she's here."

"Can I talk to her?"

"Well, she is in bed," Andrew said. "Is this urgent?"

"No, it's not really urgent. I wasn't sure if she was actually sick or just wanted to leave work early today. Well, that's it, I guess. Thanks."

Stunned, Andrew hung up the telephone. This was micromanagement on overdrive.

All employees were allowed precisely one hour for lunch. When a few of my teammates arrived seven minutes late after a birthday lunch celebration, George instituted a check-in and check-out system. Each time you left the building, you were required to write your name and the time you left the office on the clipboard posted by the front door. When you returned, you signed back in with your name and the time you returned to the office. At 25 I was back in elementary school where I needed a hall pass to go to the bathroom.

My job was wretched. I had an abysmal boss. I was disgruntled and unhappy. Each day I asked myself, "Do I quit? Do I stay and be miserable? Or do I escape and become a camp counselor?"

As you dread the thought of another day spent at work, maybe you, like me, can only see three options, or doors, to escape your misery.

Door Number One. You quit and get a new job.

Door Number Two. You stay and suffer.

Door Number Three. You escape the nine-to-five to go eat, pray, love, or become an organic lavender farmer in the South of France.*

---

* This door is also the option to take if you want to pursue your long-held dream to become an entrepreneur and start your own business. If this is you, go do it! Don't let anyone hold you back from your dreams!

On the days when I wanted to walk through Door Number Three and escape, I imagined telling George to "take this job and shove it!" I would gaze at my computer screen and dream of being a summer camp counselor at Camp Illahee in Brevard, North Carolina. I'd spend my days in the warm sunshine and cool mountain air lifeguarding on the lake. I didn't have to listen to incensed, screaming adults—only happy girls having fun. Best of all, there was not a micromanager boss in sight. I took my escape plan so far as to investigate full-time positions at Camp Illahee for me and job opportunities in Brevard for my husband, Andrew. To my dismay, there were no full-time positions available at Camp Illahee and no job prospects for Andrew. However, for about six months my getaway dream was a ray of light guaranteed to make me smile when I wanted to either scream or cry.

Over the years my pipe dream has evolved from summer camp counselor to professional nail polish namer. I imagined myself drinking wine with my girlfriends as we tried on nail polish colors and brainstormed funny nail polish names, like "Party on the Beach," "Miss Independent," or "Today I Accomplished Nothing." No bad bosses, irate clients, or mind-numbing work; just days of wine, laughter, and colorful toenails.

I think we all have some version of the "take this job and shove it" daydream. Maybe it's silly like mine, incredibly farfetched, or maybe it's the escape of retirement—a carefree life of travel, tennis, and golf with friends, or sipping tea on a veranda with a picturesque mountain view.

The reality for many retirees can be depression, isolation, and loss of identity. They have escaped the daily grind but aren't necessarily happier. Retirees who pursue part-time, temporary, or self-employment in their previous fields reported better mental and physical health than those who fully retired. Beyond the financial benefits, work can have well-being and life satisfaction benefits.[2] And according to the Sloan Center on Aging and Work and the Families and Work Institute, one in five workers has a postretirement job, and 75 percent of workers expect to work or transition to a second career at some point after they retire.

However, deep down, you and I both know that our escape fantasies are just that—daydreams that make us smile and forget the grind for a while, but probably won't lead to lasting happiness. Work has benefits beyond a paycheck. It can be a source of meaning, fulfillment, connection, and contribution.

Escaping the nine-to-five is not your only option for joy and professional gratification. And really, why would you completely abandon your career, give up your training, education, and experiences, all of which are incredibly valuable, to go find your joy elsewhere? Even people who play the lottery aren't any happier after winning millions of dollars.[3] And what guarantee do you have that your next job or next boss will be any better than your current one? There is another option. You.

It is time to own your power in the relationship with your employer so you can turn any job into your dream job.

IT TAKES TWO: THE EMPLOYER-EMPLOYEE SOCIAL CONTRACT

It's 8:17 a.m. Monday morning. You glance around your office, and a few bleary eyes, frowns, and yawns are all you can see. An "Is it Friday yet?" poster hangs on your teammate's cubicle wall. As you turn on your computer, you think, "Only eight hours and 43 minutes to go."

You are not alone. Disengagement and discontentment consume our workplaces. Only 34 percent of the workforce is engaged.[4] The current approach to address the disengagement epidemic is clearly not working. Why? Because the solutions have mostly been employer-centric and one-sided. The solutions have not acknowledged that it takes two to change a relationship: your employer *and* you. The relationship you have with your employer is a social contract. And as a social contract, *both* parties have expectations of the other party, and *both* are responsible for the health and vitality of the relationship.

The social contract with your employer can be described in terms of social exchange theory, which proposes that social behavior is the result of an exchange process. It is about give-and-take or balance and reciprocity. According to sociologist George Homans, who developed this theory, you weigh the potential benefits and risks of social relationships.[5] When the risks outweigh the rewards, you terminate or abandon the relationship. You've done this if you've ever quit a job or if you've come to work but are not really *at* work or fully engaged in your work. Your body might be at your desk, but your heart and mind are elsewhere.

You and I both know that most relationships are made up of a certain amount of give-and-take, but this does not mean that our relationships are always equal. Social exchange suggests that it is the valuing of the benefits and costs of each relationship that determines whether we choose to continue a social association. And in healthy relationships, *both* parties evaluate the benefits and costs of the relationship.

For example, let's imagine that you have a friend who is fun, outgoing, and always the life of the party. You enjoy being around this person; however, each time the bill arrives for that evening's festivities, your friend has an excuse as to why he can't pay his portion. So, you pay your friend's half of the bill as well as your own. The costs of this relationship are money, time, and effort. And the benefits are the things that you get out of this relationship: fun and companionship. As you examine the value of this relationship, you might decide that the benefits outweigh the costs or that the costs outweigh the benefits. Then, based on your decision, you will either terminate the relationship or continue it.

The exact same thing happens in your relationship with your employer. You judge the value of the benefits of the relationship with your employer, for example, compensation, intellectual stimulation, and/or the positive impact your work makes in society. You evaluate whether or not your contributions and your employer's contributions to the relationship are balanced and reciprocal. Together, these two assessments determine the health of the relationship and your commitment to the company. It is this commitment that impacts your motivation and job satisfaction, or as I would describe it, how interested, gratified, and fulfilled you are at work.

Have you ever been in a relationship where you hoped and prayed that the other person would magically change? You ask yourself, why won't he pick up his wet towel off the floor? Why does she have to talk back to the screen when we're watching a TV show?

Like she knows what a Real Housewife would do. Why won't she ever make reservations for our monthly girls' night out dinners when I know she has the OpenTable app on her phone? In the most successful relationships, people recognize that the only person they can change is themselves. And if they want the relationship to change, then the change starts first with them.

Your relationship with your employer works the same way. It is time to stop waiting, hoping, or praying for your employer to "fix" the way you're working. Change starts with you.

Of course, I understand that change is hard. It's scary. I get it. You might be thinking, "I have bills to pay and people who depend on me," "I can't go to my boss and try to make a change," or "You don't know my manager, or the company I work for." Maybe you're asking yourself: "Will 'they' question my commitment? My work ethic? Or if I try to make a change, will this jeopardize my career and destroy everything I've worked for?"

I'd like you to consider a different question: What will happen to you if you *don't* try to make a change? More of the Sunday night scaries, dreading the thought of Monday morning? More headaches, colds, and sick days? More counting down the days until the weekend? More sleepless nights of despair as you lie in bed wondering, "Is this all there is?"

So, what's possible if you *do* identify and make the changes you need to be inspired, content, and fulfilled at work? What's possible if you *do* own your career, love your work, and make your job work for you?

Joining a company does not mean abdicating your personal power. You can change the dynamic of the relationship with your employer. You have skills, experiences, and abilities that are vital and meaningful to your employer. You are the engine that fuels your

7

organization's growth. Neither your boss nor your company has all the power in the relationship. You have an equal and powerful voice.

You can be and are the catalyst for change in your life. It is up to you to identify what you need to be more satisfied, stimulated, and joyful at work. It is only then that you will be able to successfully enter into a balanced, reciprocal relationship with your employer.

DOOR NUMBER FOUR: THE PATH OF POSSIBILITY AND CHOICE

Dreading another week of cold sales calls and dealing with my ineffective boss, George, I believed that I had only three exit doors: quit, stay and suffer, or escape. Out of desperation, because none of these options were viable for me, I called my college cross-country coach, Coach Phemister, late one Sunday afternoon for guidance. He had provided wise counsel over the years, and I hoped he might have a different perspective on my miserable job.

"Carson," he asked me in his raspy, midwestern-accented voice, "In the middle of a cross-country race, do you have the power to change the racecourse?"

"Of course not," I replied.

"Right, the racecourse is fixed," Coach said. "Just because you don't want to run uphill to the finish line doesn't mean you can change the course."

He continued, "Do you remember what I told you before regionals your senior year? The only thing you can change during a race is you—your mindset, your stride, your breathing, and your self-talk. This is your power. This is how you win races, and I would suggest how you also win in life. So, what can *you* change about your job?"

Coach Phemister reacquainted me with the power of choice. I had the power to *choose* my response to people and situations, because even when I did not feel like I had any control, I always had control over myself. I hung up the phone energized, excited, and ready to walk through another door—Door Number Four.

Door Number Four is the door of choice and possibility. This is the door where you don't have to quit your job and completely give up your training, education, hard work, and investment in your career—all of which are incredibly valuable—to go find your joy and fulfillment elsewhere. You don't have to stay and suffer. Through this door, you have choice, control, and the ability to turn any job into your dream job.

When Monday morning arrived a few hours later, I walked into my office with renewed energy and hope. George was still my boss, and the check-in sheet was still posted by the door. However, I now saw that there were possibilities to create a more rewarding work environment through the power of my choices. I chose to develop my sales skills. What steps could I take to improve my outbound sales calls? What tools and resources existed to enable me to know more about the people or companies I was calling, so I could better align our services with their needs?

My first step was to ask the top salesperson in the company if I could shadow him a few times a month and listen to his outbound sales calls and join him on a few of his in-person sales meetings. Then I sat down with George and outlined my sales development plan. I asked for his feedback on the plan and for his support through scheduled daily afternoon check-ins. Within a month, he no longer came by my cubicle multiple times a day, and he stopped hovering over me during phone calls.

Four months after I leveraged the power of choice and embraced the control I had over myself, I was promoted and given the opportunity to open a new market for the company. I had walked through Door Number Four. So can you.

I know there are situations where your boss won't budge, shift, or change at all. However, you can change. There are things *you* can do. It is possible to own your career, love your work, and make your job work for you through the power of your choice. You can change how you choose to engage with your boss or how you choose to respond to him or her. There are also situations where you may choose to leave your job because it is the best next step to advance your career and fulfill your dreams. In both situations you embraced the power of choice and possibility.

Quitting, suffering, and escaping the nine-to-five are not your only options. You can turn any job into your dream job. You can walk through Door Number Four.

> I recognize that some workplaces cannot be navigated alone. If you are being harassed, bullied, or discriminated against, or are suffering from any form of mental or physical abuse in your job, the employee-employer social contract does not apply. You are not in any way responsible for any mistreatment you receive. If this is happening to you, please immediately seek outside support through your human resources department, an employee assistance program, or a trusted colleague. These situations require an immediate intervention.

STAY IN THE GAME

When you feel overwhelmed, underappreciated, unseen, and unfulfilled at work, it is hard to believe that you don't have to throw it all away. You don't have to quit or escape. In our moments of pain, suffering, and fear, it can be hard to see there are other options, much less trust that you have the power to change your professional life. You do have the power to stop running and stay in the game.

. . .

Kiri's voice was two octaves higher than usual, his cheeks had red spots, and his hands were balled into fists. He shoved his résumé across the brown, shiny conference room table as he said to me, "I'm done. I can't take it anymore. I'm quitting. Here's my résumé. What do you think?"

He was angry. We'd reached the tipping point in my client's frustration and dissatisfaction with his job. And the only solution in Kiri's mind was to quit and find another job.

I took a deep breath and hoped that Kiri might mirror my breathing and begin to calm down. "Before we begin, let's go get a cup of coffee in the breakroom."

I knew Kiri would not be able to brainstorm or think rationally when he was amped up on anger-fueled adrenaline. I needed him to walk off some of his anger because movement is one of the most effective ways to discharge and neutralize emotions.

When we returned to the conference room, I said, "Before we talk about your résumé, let's first address your anger. Anger is a no. It's our body's way of telling us that there has been some type of boundary violation. For example, think about the anger you feel when someone cuts you off in traffic. You're angry because cutting in line is not fair; you were there first. What do you think your anger might be telling you?"

He paused, the red from his cheeks finally fading, his hands now unclenched and resting on the table, and said with a loud sigh, "That I haven't had clear boundaries with the other members of the leadership team around how much time and support I can give them on their projects. And I have allowed myself to be pulled into too many different corporate projects that, while important to the company, have taken me away from my team and our responsibilities."

"And how has a lack of clear boundaries impacted you and your relationships?" I asked.

"Well, every time Robert, Karen, or Jin asks me for my opinion on a case or advice on how to approach the senior leadership to get their buy-in or to take on another joint project, I feel resentful and completely overwhelmed. I feel like I'm leading the entire division without the title or paycheck. I feel like my contributions are not fully recognized by my manager. I feel underappreciated."

"I'm curious. What's at stake if you chose to leave?"

Kiri thought about it for a few moments and then said, "Well, first my relationships with my colleagues. If I go to a competitor, they will be hurt and angry. Due to my noncompete agreement, I will have to completely change industries, which means I have to basically start my career all over again." Kiri paused and added, "I don't know if I'm willing to have any of those things happen."

I nodded and asked, "Have you ever heard the saying, 'Wherever you go, there you are'?"

"No."

"Well, what I would invite you to consider is that if you chose to leave your current job and are struggling with healthy, clear boundaries and communication here, the same situation may also occur in your new position if you don't change yourself, because there you are."

Kiri reached across the table and gently pulled his résumé back toward him, folded it in half, and put it in the spiral notebook he had laid on the table.

"So, what do you choose to do next?" I asked.

He looked me in the eye and said, "I'll start with me."

The challenges you are facing at work will not be solved by changing your work environment. A new job at a new company will be different, but *you* won't be different. If Kiri had chosen to leave, he probably would have experienced the same or a very similar situation at his new job. You must own your "piece of the action."

Over the next few months, Kiri worked on his communication skills. He identified what healthy boundaries looked and felt like with each of his colleagues. Kiri had multiple courageous conversations with each member of the leadership team and his manager to realign his contributions to their individual and corporate projects.

Six months after Kiri had thrust his résumé across the table at me, he called me on his way home early on a Friday afternoon to prepare for his daughter's birthday party that weekend. With joy and excitement in his voice, he told me he had just launched the company's first internship program, and his team had just supported the sales team in closing the largest account in the year.

Kiri took ownership and made his job work for him.

THE FIVE ESSENTIALS TO OWN, LOVE, AND MAKE YOUR JOB WORK FOR YOU

It was the final straw for me. I could not have one more conversation with a client, colleague, or friend and feel the pain of the person's despondency and dissatisfaction at work with nothing more to offer than empathy. It was time to find a solution to the disengagement epidemic that was and continues to consume us.

After confirming what our clients were telling me through my research survey, I moved on to the research on employee engagement and the employee engagement strategies our clients and other companies used. Many of them were not thinking about the relationship with their employees as a social contract of give-and-take. And many of our clients also were not thinking about the relationship with their employer this way either.

I finally saw the problem.

The employer-employee relationship is a social contract. As you've already learned, this means the employee has an equal and powerful voice to change the dynamic of the relationship. But how was I going to test my theory and ultimately find a solution? Bright spots.

I decided to find and interview people in a variety of industries and positions who were inspired, driven, and fulfilled at work. As I interviewed these bright spots, themes quickly began to emerge that aligned with what my survey research revealed and what I knew about human motivation, the motivation that drives human social behavior and humankind's search for meaning. I had the beginnings of a solution and a model. It was time to test it.

With clients who were disgruntled and demotivated, I tested what I had identified as the essential strategies and tools to turn any job into your dream job. It was trial and error because some strategies worked, and others did not. As I continued working with clients and they became more satisfied, stimulated, and content, I refined the model to what I call the five essentials to own, love, and make your job work for you: admit, align, develop, cultivate, and design.

- **Admit.** Acknowledge and ask for the recognition and appreciation due to you in exchange for your contributions.

- **Align.** Align your strengths and skills to support the accomplishment of your company's goals. Organize your work in a way that aligns with your life and the goals of the company.

- **Develop.** Develop skills and knowledge that motivate and inspire you and advance your career as well as the company.

- **Cultivate.** Cultivate authentic relationships with the team to advance your career and love your work.

- **Design.** Design your job to find meaning in your work.

Any of the strategies in any of the five essentials will move you one step closer to turning any job into the job of your dreams. The five essentials are independent of each other and do not have to be followed in a specific order. Start small and go at your own pace, because those tiny, incremental changes add up. I will show you exactly how to apply each essential to your job and encourage you along the way.

If you're like my clients, you want your work to matter, have significance, and fulfill a deeper sense of purpose. You want to use your unique strengths, skills, and talents. You want to learn, grow, and develop both professionally and personally. You want your job to fit your life. And you are no longer willing to check your humanity at the office door. You have a compelling desire to make a living *and* enjoy your life.

All of this is possible for you. I can confidently make this promise to you because I've helped thousands of our clients use the solutions, tools, and strategies in this book to do exactly that—to own, love, and make their job work for them.

The solutions outlined in the upcoming chapters have been field-tested in almost every type of business you can imagine— for-profits, nonprofits, large corporate organizations, start-ups, privately held, family-owned, publicly traded, and Fortune 100 to the Fortune 1000. I have helped teachers, physicians, consultants, accountants, lawyers, bankers, managers, individual contributors, solo entrepreneurs, analysts, and CEOs. I've helped clients whose bosses redefined what it meant to be an asshole, clients in companies that believed employees should be grateful to be paid, and clients in companies that expected you to check who you were, your values, and your sense of humanity at the front door. I know I can help you.

You don't have to quit. Your job. Your needs. Your dreams.

If you are ready to commit and join me on this journey, please email me at carson@carsontate.com, with the subject line: "I choose to make a living *and* be happy." I can't wait to hear from you and support you on what I know will be a transformational journey.

> To support you throughout your journey, I've created an Acceleration Guide on page 187. You can also download a copy of it on my website, www.carsontate.com/dreamjob.

You've taken the first step. Congratulations. Now, let's face your fears and use them so they do not derail you.

CHAPTER TWO

USE YOUR FEAR AND EMBRACE YOUR SUPERPOWERS

Every time you are tempted to react the same old way,
ask if you want to be a prisoner of the
past or a pioneer of the future.

Deepak Chopra

*F*ear. A four-letter word with significant power. It prevents you from taking that powerful step through Door Number Four. As soon as you face a challenge or adversity, you freeze right where you are. You start to question your feelings and desires. What if you fail and nothing changes? Fear of failure paralyzes you. What if you are exposed for wanting more from your career and your life? What will people think? Fear of social ostracism obstructs you. What if you continue to think work sucks, but at least it is predictable? Fear of venturing from the known to the unknown stops you.

Mark McLaughlin, a neurosurgeon and author of *Cognitive Dominance: A Brain Surgeon's Quest to Out-Think Fear*,[1] offers another perspective on fear. Fear is good. Fear, Mark McLaughlin says, forces us to pay attention. It compels us to decide and to act in the face of extremity. Fear is a survival mechanism. Fear is primal, ancient, inescapable. It drives us to make choices. Fear compels us to get clear on what matters. You can use it.

You are on a journey to transform any job into your dream job. Use your fear as a catalyst for action. It can help you clarify why your voyage matters and what's at stake if you don't choose to change how you work. Your mind is powerful and will try to keep you stuck in the "Work sucks" mantra. You can change that self-talk because you have two superpowers—choice and control—that you will unleash after you face your fears.

NAME AND CLAIM YOUR FEARS

Awake in my bed, terrified and paralyzed, I screamed for my dad. As he rushed into my bedroom, I screeched at him that Gremlins,* small, terrifying monsters, were hiding under my bed and in my closet trying to get me. Dad turned on the closet light and then shone a flashlight under the bed. There were no lurking Gremlins.

---

* The Gremlins under my bed were inspired by the 1984 movie *Gremlins*. In the movie a father buys his son a "mogwai," an adorable, cuddly animal, for Christmas. The son is warned to never expose his pet to bright light or water or to feed him after midnight. Of course, all of this happens, and this delightful, fluffy animal turns into a terrifying gang of creatures that destroy an entire city.

At age eight, all I needed was my dad and a flashlight to make my fears go away. At 44, it takes a little more to alleviate my fears. However, the first step is still the same: turn on the lights and look under your bed. Because fear thrives in the dark. Unspoken and unacknowledged, it thrives, expands, and tightens its grip on you.

When you turn on the lights and look under the bed, you name and claim your fears. This is a quick and simple process. It typically takes my clients about five minutes to complete. However, don't underestimate its power.

On a piece of paper or on a blank document on your computer or tablet, list your fears. What scares you about this journey to turn any job into your dream job? For example, what if your boss won't budge? What if your request for verbal recognition is ignored? What if your efforts to find more purpose and significance in your job fail? What if you just can't do it? Don't stop until you have listed all your fears.

Once your list is complete, look at it. These are *your* fears. Claim them. Own them. Now as you see them as they are, simply black words on a bright white piece of paper, how do you feel? Are you as afraid and overwhelmed as before? Or did your body relax slightly? When you name and claim your fears, you put yourself back in the driver's seat. Now you can use your fears.

In order to clarify why this journey to turn any job into your dream job matters, the first step is to focus on the here and now. Why? All change starts with an assessment of where you are right now—where you are beginning on your transformational journey.

Use the statements below to assess your job. Read each statement and check if the statement is true or false for you.

	TRUE	FALSE
My job is designed to enable me to use my unique skills, abilities, and strengths.		
I use my unique skills, abilities, and strengths daily.		
I have the autonomy to determine how I organize and execute on my tasks and projects.		
I have the flexibility I need to manage my professional and personal life.		
My manager recognizes and rewards me for my professional accomplishments.		
I have relationships at work that support my professional enjoyment, development, and growth.		
I have opportunities to professionally develop and grow.		
My work is a source of meaning in my life.		
I know the purpose of my work.		
My work is a source of joy in my life.		

Review your answers. This is the reality of your work today. If nothing changes, what's at stake for you? How will your mental, physical, and spiritual health, your family, friends, and significant relationships, and your community be impacted if the questions you marked false do not change?

Now let's look at the impact of *not* making changes in your day-to-day work.

For each question above that you marked false, fill in the blank for the statements below:

- I feel _____.

- I am not able to _____ for my family.

- I am not able to _____ in my career.
- I am not able to _____ in my community.
- If I don't change _____ , I will experience more of _____.
- If I don't change _____ , I will experience less _____.

Here's an example of this in action. If you marked Question 1 ("My job is designed to enable me to use my unique skills, abilities, and strengths") false, you might complete this exercise as follows:

- I feel apathetic, underutilized, invisible, unappreciated.

- I am not able to provide the income and the lifestyle I want to provide for my family.

- I am not able to be considered for training and development opportunities, get invited to participate in corporate-wide projects and initiatives, nor advance in my career.

- I am not able to donate to my synagogue in my community.

- If I don't change how I work so I can demonstrate my unique skills, abilities, and strengths, I will experience more of the same dull, uninspiring, unfulfilling, transactional work. No one will know what I am capable of and how I can make an impact in the company.

- If I don't change how I work so I can demonstrate my unique skills, abilities, and strengths, I will experience less opportunities for career advancement and professional development and less fulfillment and satisfaction in my work.

Your answers to the above questions are what's at stake if you allow fear to stop you and you don't choose to embrace your personal power to make a change and transform your job.

You know the starting point on your journey and why it vitally matters. Now let's set your intention. An intention is the sense of purpose you bring to what you do. It is the real motivation and energy behind your actions.[2] For example, my intention for this book is to empower and equip people to own, love, and make their job work for them. What is your intention? Why does taking the bold, powerful step through Door Number Four matter to you? Write or type your intention statement for the transformational journey to turn any job into the job of your dreams. Then post it where you can see it. You now have a strong, visible reminder of your personal power and why this journey matters to you.

Just because you have an intention statement does not mean that you will not still feel fear. You will. Feel that fear. Then, with courage, take the next step toward your dreams. As I heard Oprah Winfrey say when I attended her 2020 Vision Tour in Charlotte, North Carolina, "The true meaning of courage is to be afraid—and then, with your knees knocking and your heart racing, take the leap anyway."[3] You can do this. You will not allow anything to stand between you and your dream. Not even your mind, which wants to keep you stuck in the familiar refrain of "Work sucks."

HOW YOUR MIND IS KEEPING YOU STUCK IN A "WORK SUCKS" REFRAIN

As I nervously stepped into my first class as a college freshman, the first thing I saw was Professor Lorig. His hair and full beard were salt and pepper gray. Thick, round, black-framed glasses made his eyes look unnaturally large. His houndstooth tweed jacket with brown patches on the elbows was hanging over the back of a chair. And even though it was early September, he had on blue wool socks with his Birkenstocks. "Oh," I thought to myself, "he looks like a college professor."

Has this ever happened to you: you meet someone, and they look just like the picture you had of them in your mind? Or you talk to someone on the phone, never having seen their face, and when you meet them in person, you think to yourself that their voice fits them?

Why does this happen? Because of mental models, or schemas. I define a schema as a mental concept that informs what you can expect from a variety of experiences and situations. Schemas are developed based on information from your life experiences and then stored in your memory.

Your brain creates these mental models, or schemas, because they make it easier and faster to process and make sense of the millions of images, sounds, words, and smells that flood our senses every day. When I saw Professor Lorig for the first time, my brain rapidly absorbed the visual image of him and then matched it up with the schema I had in my brain for "college professor." While helpful at times, mental models can keep us stuck in old patterns and old beliefs.

We all have mental models about work and being an employee. Many of these were formed early in life as we watched our family members, teachers, and other adults in our lives go to work. Some of these mental models may be neutral, like the one I had about college professors, but others can be positive or negative. All of these have conditioned us with beliefs about work. Our goal is to change the negative mental models we currently have that keep us stuck, unfulfilled, and disengaged at work.

To create the professional life you want and change what you have been conditioned to negatively believe about work, your first step is to pay attention to your brain in action. For example, when you drive your car to work, you turn on a specific sequence and combination of neurological networks. These networks are clusters of neurons that work together as a community because you've done that particular action numerous times. Each time you drive your car to work, the "how to drive a car" community of neurons fire together. According to neuroscientist Dr. Joe Dispenza, the more you repeat a thought, choice, behavior, experience, or emotion, the more those neurons fire and wire together and the more they will remain intertwined.[4]

When you keep thinking the same negative thoughts about work such as "I can't be happy at my company," "No one recognizes and rewards me for my knowledge and contributions," "I don't have any control over my time or my work," or "I'm not challenged," you hardwire your brain into a "Work sucks" pattern even if these thoughts are true only some of the time.

The problem is that your brain becomes an artifact of your past thinking. It becomes easier to automatically think in the same habitual ways than to challenge your past assumptions. And if you repeatedly feel the same emotions over and over again (like anger, fear, frustration, or sadness), it's like you've added superglue to these patterns. According to Dispenza, emotions are the language of the body, so when you combine emotions with your negative thoughts, you are conditioning your body into the past.[5] And this makes it very difficult to be joyful, fulfilled, and engaged in the present moment at work.

So, what does this look like in your life? It's Monday morning and your alarm jolts you awake. Your first thought is, "Ugh, it's Monday again, and I have to go back to work". You get out of bed, and immediately your thoughts are on overdrive. Work is boring, your boss doesn't appreciate you, your cube mate is a complete jerk, and the breakroom smells. These thoughts are so deeply wired with emotions that before you even brush your teeth, anxiety, irritation, and/or sadness floods your body.

Then, as you continue your morning and make your coffee, dress, and drive your usual route to work, the negativity continues. When you arrive, you turn on your computer, grab your notebook, and head to the conference room for your first meeting of the day—which you dread. Meetings, email, more meetings, and more email fill your day until it's time to go home. You drive home the exact same route you took to work. You cook the same food for dinner, watch a TV show, and get ready for bed like you always do—wash your face, brush your teeth, and put on your pajamas. Then you get in bed and turn out the lights. The day is over, and tomorrow it starts all over again.

If you repeatedly do the same routines, they will become a habit. Dispenza defines a habit as a "redundant set of automatic, unconscious thoughts, behaviors, and emotions that you acquire through frequent repetition."[6] The result? You are living on autopilot. You're unaware of what you're doing and why.

How often don't you remember your drive to work because you were rehashing in your head what your boss said to you two days ago? Or maybe you email and text while talking to a colleague and later in the day forget what you agreed to do for her. These unconscious behaviors prevent you from living in the present moment. And because you are not in the present moment, but mired in the past, you are keeping your dreams and goals out of your reach, asserts Dispenza.[7] You can't create a work environment that contributes to your contentment, joy, and engagement.

However, once you are aware of your unconscious behaviors, you can create your new future instead of dreaming of escape.

It's time to stop just "getting through the day" so you can make it to happy hour on Friday afternoon. Stuck in the past, existing in an endless loop of negative thoughts, is no way to live—especially if your autopilot runs on the emotions of fear, sadness, or unworthiness.

You want to own, love, and make your job work for you, and you have everything you need inside you to make this a reality. Your next step is to identify where you may have forgotten that you—and only you—have the power to transform your job into the job of your dreams.

YOUR SUPERPOWERS:
CHOICE AND CONTROL

"You've forgotten your superpowers," I said to Yvette, my coaching client and the chief operating officer of a large transportation company. As soon as the words left my lips, I cringed. Who talks to executives about superpowers? Even though we had worked together for six months, she was going to think I had completely lost my mind.

Yvette's business and team had grown rapidly, and with that growth came challenges. However, Yvette was not leading, nor navigating the difficulties well. Yvette blamed the challenges with the West Coast expansion on the tight labor market in California and her challenges with Sundeep, the CFO, by telling me he did not like working with women.

Yvette was trapped in a downward spiral. She had what psychologist Julian Rotter calls an *external locus of control.* Yvette believed that her success or failure was controlled by other people, environmental factors, chance, or fate—and she was stuck. She was so stuck that she considered quitting. She couldn't see how she had choice and/or control in each of these situations.

It was time for Yvette to lean into her superpowers: choice and control. Why? Because these superpowers imbue you with the confidence and knowledge that the only person you can change is yourself. They enable you to be a victor in your life. Victors have what Rotter calls an *internal locus of control* and believe that their success or failure is due to their own efforts. Victors know that their power is through the choices they make and the control they take over their lives. They know that they are in the driver's seat of their life. And they know that they "have a piece of the action," as my dear friend Gail likes to say.

You and only you can change your life. You have the power. You have the knowledge, skills, and ability to create the professional life you want. You have the superpowers of choice and control. It's time for you to dust them off and own their strength. It's a waste to spend time and energy blaming your office's culture, technology, your boss, your industry, market conditions, your team members, your commute, or the drab office building you work in as the reason or reasons you're not satisfied, stimulated, and engaged at work.

● ● ●

After I blurted out that Yvette had forgotten her superpowers, I asked: "Where have you succumbed to believing that you don't have a choice and everything is out of your control?"

As she sat back in her white leather chair, resting on the pink fringed cushion that took up most of her seat, Yvette burst into tears. "Carson, it was easier to just blame all of the problems on everyone and everything else. It's scary, hard, and overwhelming to face the fact that I have both contributed to the challenges and must be part of the solution. It was just easier to abdicate the power of my choice and control in each of these situations."

Yvette sat silently for a moment with her tissue in her hand. Then she said, "I've been telling myself a lot of stories.

"The story I'm telling myself about Deon, who leads the West Coast, is that he is so new he doesn't really know what to do," she continued. "Also, I think I can do it better. And Sundeep, well, I find him abrasive and arrogant, so I have limited my interactions with him, which I see now has only made our accounting situation worse."

As soon as Yvette said out loud how she had contributed to her company's challenges, she brought them into the light. We had cracked the armor she had put up to protect her ego. To paraphrase Leonard Cohen, "Cracks are where the light can shine into places that are dark, scary, and vast."[8] Now she could see the stories for what they were—excuses to protect her ego and sense of self. In the light, they did not appear so overwhelming.

"Yvette," I said, "Often it is fear that is keeping us stuck. And fear is nothing more than a lack of faith. What do you lack faith in?"

A fresh stream of tears rolled down Yvette's face as she said, "What if I'm not good enough? What if I don't know what will work on the West Coast? What if I can't train Deon, and what if I can't work through my dislike of Sundeep?"

It was the familiar refrain of "Am I worthy?" and "Am I good enough?" I had asked myself this too many times to count. And I had heard it from every one of my clients at least once during a coaching engagement.

"So, what do you want to do now? What is one step you can take to know that you are good enough? And what is one step you can take to start to address each of the challenges you are facing?"

Yvette paused for a moment and said, "First, I'm going to go back to my five-minutes-a-day journaling practice where I write down three things I'm grateful for, five things that I did well that day, and one insight I had about my leadership. I found this very helpful when I did it every day. I'll journal before I leave the office each afternoon. I will also schedule a meeting with Sundeep to discuss how I can help his team achieve its goals and meet with Deon and develop a training plan for him so I can teach him how to lead his team."

Yvette had claimed her superpowers. She was a victor in her life.

Now, let's claim your superpowers so you can be a victor in your life.

We'll use the same steps Yvette followed to recognize and unlock your superpowers.

Unlock Your Superpowers: Step 1

The first step to unlock your superpowers is to sharpen your powers of self-awareness. This is your ability to observe your own behavior. One of the most powerful ways for you to become both the observer and the observed is through introspection and reflection. Reflect on the following questions:

- What resistance do you have to being curious about your own behavior? What do you need to support you as you become an explorer of your own behavior?

- What have you noticed triggers you to a place of "Work sucks"?

- When you are in this place of "Work sucks," what do you feel? Where do you feel it in your body? How would you describe your emotions or emotional state?

- When you are in this place of "Work sucks," are you in a specific situation? Does it occur with specific people? Does it occur at a specific time of the day, week, or month? What specific external conditions are present?

- How can you become more self-aware? For example, ask yourself throughout your day, "How am I feeling right now? What do I think might be driving that feeling?"

It can be helpful to come back to these questions as you read the rest of this book to continue to hone your ability to be self-aware. Self-awareness is an essential skill for you to turn any job into your dream job.

Unlock Your Superpowers: Step 2

The second step to unlock your superpowers is to recognize that you are in the driver's seat of your life. You exert your power through the choices you make and the control you take over your life. Reflect on the following questions to identify where you have abdicated your power:

- Where have you blamed your professional dissatisfaction on other people or situations?

- Where have you ignored or denied your professional discontent, frustration, or unhappiness rather than acknowledge it to yourself?

- What has been the impact on you mentally, physically, emotionally, and/or spiritually when you have abdicated your personal power?

Once you recognize that you have renounced your superpowers of choice and control, you are ready for the third step: to explore the stories you tell yourself.

Unlock Your Superpowers: Step 3

Stories are tricks of the ego to maintain your self-esteem. However, they do the opposite. They keep you stuck in a powerless state that undermines and slowly erodes your confidence. Think about the questions below to help you identify the stories that are keeping you stuck:

- What's the story you're telling yourself about your job?

- What's the story you're telling yourself about your relationship with your boss, coworkers, or teammates?

- What's the story you're telling yourself about the projects you work on, your position in the company, and your influence within the organization?

- What's the story you're telling yourself about your professional development, growth, and career advancement opportunities?

- What's the story you're telling yourself about the value, meaning, and purpose in your work?

Now that you have identified your stories, the final step is to face your fears one more time.

Unlock Your Superpowers: Step 4

In this step you will explore how fear, or a lack of faith in yourself, prevents you from claiming your superpowers. Reflect on the four questions below to address the lack of faith you have in yourself and identify how you can overcome your fears:

- What do you lack faith in that prevents you from believing that you can change your professional life?

- Is the root of your fear in the prior question, "Am I worthy?" Or "Am I good enough?"

- What will it take for you to be the victor in your life?

- What will you do to embrace your superpowers of choice and control?

You are ready. Now is the time to let your superpowers shine.

. . .

Fear compels you to get clear on what matters. Use it as a catalyst for action. Let it focus your head and heart on why your journey to transform your job matters and what is at stake if you don't choose to change how you work. You have superpowers—choice and control. No one can take them away from you. You are always at choice. You control how you think and act. Everything you need is inside you *right now* to turn an unfulfilling, unhappy work life into a vibrant, significant, joyful one. Allow your superpowers to shine brightly so you can create the job of your dreams.

Walk confidently through Door Number Four.

STEP ONE

OWN IT.

ACKNOWLEDGE WHO YOU ARE AND WHAT YOU NEED

ADMIT your recognition and appreciation needs

ALIGN your strengths

YOUR DREAM JOB

| ADMIT | ALIGN | DEVELOP | CULTIVATE | DESIGN |

YOUR SKILLS + EXPERIENCES + VALUES

CHAPTER THREE

ADMIT YOUR RECOGNITION AND APPRECIATION NEEDS

Patti and I stood on a large brick patio soaking up the sunshine during a break from the writer's conference. We were talking about this book and what being fulfilled, content, and stimulated looked like for both of us when she told me about the first 14 years of her professional career.

"I helped them grow from a small start-up through the sale of the company to a globally esteemed brand," Patti said. "I got to work early, stayed late, and even dreamed about how to market our product—anything to support the company. But I only remember my manager saying thank you for my contributions and hard work a few times."

"How demoralizing and difficult."

"It was. I felt like the company was just as much mine as it was Bill's, the owner. But my manager did not see me. He rarely acknowledged my contributions and offered only a few paltry words of praise of my performance. I was miserable. I had to drag myself into work. I got tired of not feeling valued or appreciated."

It was hard to imagine Patti like that because the woman standing before me had a light in her eyes, flashed an easy smile, and had laughed throughout the opening keynote that morning.

"Well, if you're at this conference, I think I know what happened. You left the company, didn't you?" I asked.

"Yes, I finally left the company. All I wanted and needed to hear was thank you more often."

Patti moved on. However, that is not *your* only option.

．．．

Remember, you just walked through Door Number Four, the door of possibility and choice, where you own, love, and make your job work for you. You did the courageous, powerful work to prepare for your transformational journey to turn your job into your dream job. Now your journey begins. Your first step is to own it. To admit to yourself and your company that you need credit and gratitude for the knowledge, skills, and contributions you make in the relationship with your employer. And to take responsibility for your appreciation needs being met at work. Patti knew that she needed to hear thank you, but she never voiced how disheartening it was to feel unappreciated. She suffered in silence. You don't have to. You can do something different.

You can acknowledge, identify, and ask for the appreciation and thankfulness due to you in exchange for your contributions. How do you do that? Focus on your self-esteem. It impacts your performance, confidence, and willingness to ask for your recognition needs to be met.

CULTIVATE POSITIVE SELF-ESTEEM
AT WORK THROUGH FEEDBACK

You spend about one-third of your life at work. So, it's pretty obvious that what happens at work and how you experience your job can positively or negatively affect your self-esteem. Think about how you feel when your boss forwards a complimentary email from a client to the entire division. Or how you feel when you falter in a presentation and the leadership team doesn't approve your project. Work can be a roller-coaster ride of emotional highs and lows.

Your experiences at work affect what researchers Pierce, Gardner, Cummings, and Dunham define as organizational self-esteem. It is the degree to which you consider yourself capable, significant, and worthy as an organization member.[1] When you believe that you make a difference in your company, that you are a valued team member and are competent, you are more content, gratified, and joyful at work.

So, what can you do to enhance your self-esteem? Create more opportunities for positive, successful work experiences by asking for feedback.

. . .

Annette was five feet tall only in her favorite pair of heels. Always dressed in an edgy pantsuit fresh off the runways of New York, she was quick to smile, laugh, and stop in the hallway to chat with team members. Her CEO, Paul, was being pressured by the board, and Wall Street, to address the significant lack of diversity not only on his leadership team but throughout the organization. Annette was the second highest ranking woman at the $3.3 billion global company and the only woman to ever be considered to lead a billion-dollar business unit.

With 25 years of experience in the industry, her extensive knowledge of the business, and a powerful ability to negotiate a profitable deal with the most challenging, intractable clients, it appeared that Annette would be the business unit's new president when the current president, John, retired at the end of the next fiscal year. However, Paul had doubts.

"John, I don't think Annette can replace you. Every time I ask her a question about the business, she launches into these long-winded, rambling answers filled with unnecessary details. I want to yell at her and say, "Make a point. State an opinion. Be succinct." I think she is too bogged down in operations to think strategically. I'm not willing to put her on an earnings call with Wall Street, nor have her represent me at an industry conference," Paul said.

John shared Paul's feedback with Annette, and John agreed to her request for an executive coach.

At our first coaching session, I told Annette, "I can help you think through how to communicate succinctly, strategically, and impactfully. We can role-play during our coaching sessions. However, I can't provide the real-time feedback that is necessary to change your behavior. You are going to have to ask John and your colleagues for feedback."

Annette's eyes widened, and she took a take a deep breath as soon as I mentioned the word *feedback*. Asking for feedback is hard. It doesn't matter how much experience you have, or your position in the company, or how skilled you are. It's scary. We all sweat when we solicit and receive feedback.

I can still remember the first time my manager, Mark, said to me, "Carson, can I give you some feedback?" My stomach churned and my hands started to sweat. Immediately my brain went to the worst-case scenario—"I'm going to get fired!" The lack of certainty around what was coming next created so much unease that I still cannot recall what Mark said to me that afternoon.

Real-time, specific feedback is one of the most effective ways to change your behavior and optimize your performance. It is also one of the most powerful methods you have to create more affirmative, successful work experiences. When you feel capable, confident, and valued, you have higher self-esteem.

In order to reduce and eliminate feedback anxiety, there are three strategies to use when you ask for and receive feedback: employ a growth mindset, proactively ask for the feedback, and use the SEE framework—specific, example, explain. Let's dive into each strategy a little deeper...

Feedback Strategy #1: Employ a Growth Mindset

Carol Dweck, a psychology professor at Stanford University, discovered a simple but groundbreaking concept after decades of study: the power of mindset. Through her research, she demonstrated that the view, or mindset, you adopt for yourself profoundly affects how you lead your life. Your success at work can be dramatically influenced by how you think about your talents and abilities.

Dweck identified two types of mindset: fixed and growth. People with a fixed mindset believe that their intelligence and abilities are fixed. People with a growth mindset believe that

43

intelligence can be developed, that the brain is a muscle that can be trained. This leads to the desire to improve, embrace challenges, persist in the face of setbacks, see effort as the path to mastery, and learn from criticism.[2] A growth mindset is instrumental to create more affirmative, efficacious work experiences.

A growth mindset enables you to train your brain to understand that feedback—even negative feedback—is constructive. You want to get better. It allows the possibility that you might have a blind spot. You acknowledge that the feedback is not personal. It's not an attack on your self-esteem. It is a way to improve your performance. With a growth mindset, you don't have to link negative feedback to your identity.

Feedback is an opportunity for you to learn a new skill. To employ a growth mindset, you acknowledge and embrace your imperfections, value the process of professional development, and replace the word *failing* with *learning*. Your action step to make this happen: the next time you ask for feedback, tell yourself that it is for your development, growth, and advancement. Remind yourself that with this feedback you will be able to generate more successful, positive work experiences.

Feedback Strategy #2: Proactively Ask for Feedback

When you *ask* for feedback, you put yourself in a psychological state that is ready to receive negative news. This is important because *unsolicited feedback* can activate the social threat response. If you feel threatened, you won't be ready to receive, retain, or agree with the feedback you receive. When you solicit feedback, you minimize this threat response. You also have more autonomy and certainty when you ask for feedback because you focus the conversation where it will be the most useful for you. The person you've requested it from also benefits because you have given clear guidelines on the specific feedback you want. As a result, the information you receive is more relevant and less threatening to your status, and the entire conversation feels more equitable and fair.[3]

Feedback Strategy #3: Use the SEE Framework

Now that you know how to mentally prepare to ask for feedback, your likely next question is *how* to ask for it. I came up with a framework, SEE, to help my clients effectively ask for feedback:

- **Be *specific*.** Ask for the specific type of feedback that you want to receive.

- **Share an *example*.** Provide an example of the type of feedback you want to receive.

- ***Explain*.** Ask the person you requested feedback from to explain what you did or did not do.

Let's look at how Annette used the SEE framework with her manager, John.

Annette asked John for specific feedback on her ability to communicate clearly and succinctly during her presentations to the senior leadership team.

She then shared an example of the type of feedback she wanted to receive by asking him to tell her when he did not hear the bottom line or her central point within the first three sentences of her presentations.

Finally, Annette asked John to tell her at what point he did hear the bottom line or central point during her presentations. Because she asked John to explain when in her presentations she shared the bottom line, she knew exactly how to adjust her communication style to be more clear and succinct. There are three additional things to do when you ask for feedback:

- Ask for specific feedback from your peers and colleagues to ensure a well-rounded perspective.

- Ask for feedback often. The more frequently you ask, the faster you can change your behavior.

- Ask for feedback immediately. You'll reduce the time between the event and the feedback you receive so the person's memory is fresh and you don't suffer from revisionist history.

● ● ●

When I walked into Annette's office four months later, I expected to find her jet-lagged and gripping a large cup of coffee. She'd just returned from her industry's global conference in London the prior morning. Instead of dragging herself out of her chair when I arrived at her office door, Annette leaped up, grinning from ear to ear. Her eyes sparkled, and she had the relaxed look of someone who had just come back from a spa.

"Carson, the conference went better than I could have ever imagined! In two days, I succinctly and confidently responded to questions from 23 different industry CEOs. At the cocktail reception, a CEO who was in one of my one-on-one industry updates cornered me. All he wanted to talk about was us acquiring his firm! Paul has been pursuing him for 18 months, and he called me this morning and told me he had heard how well I did and looked forward to talking to the CEO about an acquisition."

Annette had represented her company, her division, and herself with authority, credibility, and confidence. Without feedback it would not have been possible. Eighteen months later Annette was promoted.

OVERRIDE YOUR BRAIN'S NEGATIVITY BIAS

It can be hard to believe you're valuable, and even tougher to ask to be recognized for your contributions when you're stuck on an endless repeat of your mistakes and bad work experiences. It's easy to get stuck in the vortex of negative ruminations. Why? Because of the brain's "negativity bias." Your brain is simply hardwired for a greater sensitivity to unpleasant news.[4] While this may have served us well thousands of years ago when we had to avoid rampaging predators and rival tribes, today this negativity erodes confidence and self-esteem, which can make it difficult to use your strengths to achieve your goals. You can't get recognized if your performance is subpar.

It's time to override your brain's negativity bias.

. . .

Dark circles under his eyes, scrubs rumpled, Jerome was on his second cup of coffee—and his tenth negative comment. He'd been on call last night, and it was busy. Twenty minutes into our coaching session, I said, "Jerome, have you noticed that we spend most of our coaching sessions with you telling me all your mistakes, screwups, and missteps? I hear about conversations with colleagues, nurses, and administrators where you did not communicate clearly, how you got angry during a surgery and snapped at your nurse, or about the email you sent with typos. Rarely do I hear anything positive."

"As a physician, I'm trained to evaluate my performance, especially my mistakes so I can learn from them," he said.

"And what happens when all you think about is your mistakes, especially on your drive home from work?"

"Well, obviously, I overlook where I have improved my communication skills, which is what we are working on," Jerome replied. "But I think it's starting to impact my family. When I get home from work, I'm depressed, angry, frustrated, and disappointed in myself. And I take it out on Elaine and the boys. I'll shout at Elaine and the boys, then retreat to my office for the rest of the evening."

"Would you be open to a strategy to stop rehashing every mistake, slight, and negative event from your day on your commute home so you don't shout at Elaine and the boys?"

"Of course."

"On your way home from work, at each red stoplight, answer out loud two questions: What was one win today? And what did I do to contribute to that win? The stoplight is your trigger to identify a positive work experience. Saying your win out loud halts your negative self-talk and reinforces the positive work experience."

Jerome furrowed his brow, raised an eyebrow, and looked at me as though I had just suggested a woo-woo pop psychology idea from the self-help aisle at the bookstore.

I explained to Jerome that the research on using self-affirmations, what I had asked him to do on his drive home from work, showed it could enhance his problem solving under stress and enable him to separate who he is as a person from his mistakes and missteps.[5]

After a long pause, he said, "Well, what I'm doing now isn't working. So I'll try it."

Over the next few months Jerome used the stoplights on his drive home from work as his reminder to speak aloud a positive work experience. The first few weeks he only did it a few times. As he realized that there were more wins than failures, his confidence improved, and he worked harder on being an impactful, persuasive communicator and leader. By the fourth month, he was using the strategy every day.

About six months later, I received a text from Jerome's wife, Elaine. She said, "Thank you for your work with Jerome. He's happier, more relaxed, and the boys can't wait for him to get home." I also received a text from Jerome. He had been named the new medical director of the Pediatric Cardiology division.

What can you do to stop the endless loop of negative thoughts? Here are seven strategies to override your brain's negativity bias so you can leverage your strengths to achieve your goals and be appreciated for your accomplishments. Each one can be implemented in less than five minutes. You don't need to use all of them to flip your brain's switch from negative to positive. Choose the one strategy that is the easiest for you to implement.

Negativity Bias Strategy #1:
Rehearse Good News and Share It

You walk through the door at the end of the day, and the first thing out of your mouth is what went wrong today. The barista messed up your coffee order, the staff meeting went an hour long, there was an accident on the highway, you were stuck in traffic for 45 minutes, and your friend didn't text you back. Before you know it, you've spent most of the evening telling your spouse, partner, significant other, or friend everything that went wrong during your day.

You're fixated on the negative.

Simply flip your brain's negative script and instead share only the good things that happened to you during the day. Your mind needs practice focusing on the positive. Share your good news first. Walk into your home and let the first words out of your mouth be the three positive things that happened during the day.

Negativity Bias Strategy #2:
Share Two Roses and a Thorn

Every night at dinner, each member of our family shares two roses and one thorn from the day. The roses are positive events, experiences, or feelings from our day, and the thorn is the negative. This is a great way for our entire family to focus on the good in our lives. We also learn about each other's days. And there are many evenings after we've shared our two roses that we realize we don't have a thorn and we'll add an additional rose.

Use this simple framework to help you identify your successes or enjoyable events from your day. Ask your family, a friend, or a colleague to do this with you so you have the accountability and support to do this daily. Remember, your mind needs practice to focus on the positive.

Negativity Bias Strategy #3: Break the Cycle

Someone cuts in front of you in line for coffee and pretends they didn't see you. You get mad. Then when you step up to the counter to place your order, you snap at the barista. Negative experiences are sticky and often lead to further negative experiences. Break this cycle. The next time someone is rude, upsets you, or cuts you off in traffic, forgive them in the moment. The easiest way to do this is to assume honorable intent and then reframe the situation.

Let's use someone cutting you off in traffic as an example. In order to break the cycle, you first assume honorable intent and say to yourself that if they had another option, they would have made a different choice. Then reframe the situation. Imagine they've received a phone call from the hospital and their family member is in the emergency room. How would you react? They didn't cut you off to ruin your day. They cut you off because they were frantically trying to get to the hospital.

Sure, there will be times when you are so mad you can't break the cycle. I get it. Give yourself a pass and try again. Your goal is to realize when one negative event is adversely impacting future events and then to break the cycle.

Negativity Bias Strategy #4:
Feed the Positive

What you focus on becomes your reality. Your thoughts can and do dictate your experiences. So, focus on and feed the positive. How can you do this? A few ideas are to dictate or write down three to five pleasant things that happened to you during the day. Keep thank you notes, affirmations, or words of praise from your clients, boss, or colleagues and refer to them when you feel yourself caught in a downward spiral of "you suck."

I personally have a folder in my office labeled "Get Out of Your Funk." In it I keep emails from our clients on how we've helped them, their teams, or their organization. I also add cards from my team, praise from previous bosses, and thank you notes in this folder. When that negative voice chirps in my ear, I pull out this file so I can focus on an accomplishment or a positive experience from the past. It counteracts the powerful vortex of negative emotions and validates that I've been successful in the past, which makes it easier to imagine myself successful in the future.

Negativity Bias Strategy #5:
Keep a Report Card on Your Best Efforts

Review your to-do list at the end of the day, and next to each completed task, note the effort you put into it. For example, 50 percent, 80 percent, or 100 percent effort. Identify your top three best effort tasks and write or type them on a new list called "Best Efforts." Add to your "Best Efforts" list each day for a week. By the end of the week, you'll have 15 reminders of your efforts and positive work experiences so you can override your brain's negativity bias. If you can't think of anything positive you've done, ask a trusted colleague to share how you've supported them or one of their projects this week.

Negativity Bias Strategy #6:
Notice When You're Negative

Notice and identify when you're focused more on the negative. Is there a day, a week, or even a month that you notice you're more negative than positive? Is there a time of day you're more inclined to fixate on the negative? Or are there projects that tend to bring out the Debbie Downer in you? To change your behavior, the first step is to be aware of when your brain concentrates on the negative. You can't change what you are not aware of in your life. Once you're cognizant of your patterns, you can decide to do something differently.

To shift your negative thoughts and emotions, use movement, music, humor, fellowship, or affirmations. For example, walk the halls in your office, listen to your favorite song, watch a silly cat video on YouTube, talk to a friend or colleague, or state an affirmation such as "I made a mistake and I'll learn from it." Identify which one works best for you; then use it the next time you find yourself at 9:27 a.m. on a Monday morning stuck in the negative mental quagmire of "I am terrible at my job."

Negativity Bias Strategy #7:
Focus on Solving Problems

If you're caught in the swirl of negative thoughts, focus on solving problems. Use a visual reminder to help your brain shift gears from negativity to problem solving. Make a stop sign and post it on your desk or computer or change your phone screen saver to a stop sign. The stop sign reminds you that you can control your thinking and change the story you are currently telling yourself. Every time a negative thought pops up, look at the stop sign and say, "Stop." Ask yourself, what would a successful, confident person do right now to solve this the problem? Then do it!

· · ·

To be recognized for your contributions at work, you must believe that you're valuable. Override your brain's negativity bias. Focus on your positive work experiences.

TAKE OWNERSHIP FOR
YOUR RECOGNITION NEEDS

When I interview potential new team members, I always ask them to describe their best day at work. Their responses typically include an accomplishment and a form of acknowledgment. For example, "I planned our employee summit, and my manager told me that it was the best summit the firm had ever sponsored," or "I figured out why the tax withholdings were not calculating correctly on one of our employee's paychecks and she received a refund. She sent me an email thanking me for my help."

As a manager, I listen to hear what types of experiences contribute to a potential employee's best day at work and the form of recognition and praise that is important to the person. When

I hired my chief of staff, Wendelyn, she described her best day as finally placing a new team member for an extremely difficult client. In front of the entire team, her manager thanked her for her hard work and praised her for finding the exceptional candidate. Wendelyn needs and wants verbal praise, preferably in front of her colleagues. This is how she prefers to be appreciated for her efforts.

How do you want to be recognized for your accomplishments at work? Do you need verbal praise, or do you want written praise, or do you prefer your name on a plaque on the wall? Do you want to be acknowledged in front of your peers, senior leadership, or the entire firm for your achievements? Or are you like Patti, whom I met at the writer's conference, who prefers a quiet "Thank you for your hard work"?

To identify how you want to be seen and praised for your contributions, reflect, journal, or talk to a friend or colleague about each of the following questions:

- What was your best day at work? If you can't think of a best day at work, can you think about a time when you were seen and valued for your contributions? Maybe this was when you volunteered at a nonprofit, served on a committee at your child's school, or were a member of an athletic team.

- What happened?

- What did you do?

- How did you feel?

- What type of praise and recognition did you receive?

Be honest with yourself as you consider each question. Once you have answered each question, look for any themes or trends in your answers. This is how you want to receive acknowledgment.

We all want and need to be seen and valued. To desire praise does not mean that you are egocentric or arrogant or that you are not a team player. Appreciation for your contributions is integral to being content at work. If you are not clear on how you need to be affirmed, how can your manager recognize you in a way that supports your self-esteem and makes you feel valuable? I would argue that your manager can't.

Ask for What You Need

Once you are clear on your needs, the next step is to determine how to get them met in your job. This is where you will feel the fear and do it anyway. When I coach our clients to ask to have their acknowledgment needs met, most of them look at me with terror in their eyes. They often say what you may be thinking: "What will my manager think of me when I ask for what I need to be appreciated and valued?" I'll offer you the response I always give my clients: "What will happen if you don't ask? More of the same?"

The best way to ask for what you need is to connect it to elevating your performance. This moves the spotlight from you to your impact in the organization. And it can neutralize some of your fears. Use the same SEE feedback model you used to receive feedback on your performance—be specific, use an example, and explain. In this situation, you are specific about the type of recognition and praise that you need, you provide an example of what this looks like, and you explain how you would like to receive it.

. . .

Andy was newly promoted and leading a team for the first time. He was excited and gratified that the firm saw his potential and hired me as a coach to help him transition into his new role. A few months into our coaching engagement, Andy told me that he had begun to feel unrecognized and underappreciated. I was surprised. I asked him what had changed.

"I really don't know. I didn't feel this way when Rylan was my manager," he replied.

"What did Rylan do differently than Sahil, your new manager?"

"Well, she set clear expectations of me and the team. And she praised my contributions and accomplishments," he said.

"Which of these does Sahil do?"

"He sets clear expectations of me and the team. But he hasn't noticed my contributions, nor any of my accomplishments. We brought in a new client three weeks ago, and he still has not said anything to me about it!"

"Would you like him to recognize your contributions and accomplishments?"

"Of course," Andy replied. "But how do I get him to do that?"

I thought for a minute. "How about this: Sahil knows that communication and delegation skills are the focus of our coaching. Have you considered asking him to support your professional development? What if you asked him to verbally acknowledge you for a specific behavior tied to one of your coaching goals? It could be as simple as Sahil telling you that you did a great job being clear and concise, which are two of your coaching communication goals," I said.

"I can't ask him to tell me I did a great job. This isn't Little League baseball, and I'm not 12," Andy said.

"I understand. It can be scary to admit you have a need and to ask for it. However, what happens if you don't ask?"

Andy narrowed his eyes at me, pressed his lips together, and scrunched his shoulders up to his ears. Resistance and fear had set in. At our next coaching session, a month later, I asked Andy how things were going with Sahil.

"Well, I finally took your advice. Sahil told me he wanted to support my leadership development and immediately started acknowledging when I communicated or delegated effectively."

Andy took the courageous step to ask for the praise and affirmation he needed. So can you.

Rehearse the Conversation

The final step to take ownership for your recognition needs is to rehearse the conversation you want to have with your manager with a friend or colleague. This will trick your brain into thinking that you've already had the conversation. So, when it's time to ask your manager to meet your needs, your brain thinks you're having the conversation for a second time, not the first.

You cannot assume that your manager knows how to acknowledge your accomplishments. If you are not recognized in a way that is meaningful to you, it is up to you identify your specific needs and ask to have them met. The goal is authentic appreciation. You need to be seen and valued for the person you are and the contributions you make to your company. Remember that we are all unique individuals with diverse appreciation needs.

You may need verbal praise or written affirmations or tangible gifts like time off or tickets to your local sports team's home game. Maybe it's quality time with your manager or a colleague where you can catch up, share your ideas, and have their focused attention and a quality conversation. Or you may feel valued when your manager or others on your team reach out and help you or when they work alongside you on a difficult project. Appreciation and recognition are not one-size-fits-all. They are personal. You are on a transformational journey to turn any job into your dream job. It is up to you to be clear on your distinct appreciation needs and then ask for what you need.

SHOW ME THE MONEY

My husband, Andrew, and I have watched the movie *Jerry Maguire* so many times I've lost count. If you haven't seen the film, Tom Cruise plays Jerry, a sports agent who leaves a highly paid position at his firm to found his own values-based company. Our favorite scene is when professional football player Rod Tidwell, played by Cuba Gooding Jr., tells Jerry to "show me the money!" Rod wants more money. He also wants the respect and recognition afforded to professional football players who receive high salaries for their performance on the field.

At certain points in your career, and maybe even right now, you too may have had moments where you wanted to shout, "Show me the money!" And understandably so! You want to be financially rewarded for your skills and contributions that enable the company to be profitable. Money is the currency of appreciation in our world. It is one way companies can express their appreciation for the job you perform.

If you've ever found out that a colleague whose job is the same as or similar to yours is making more money than you, you've probably felt worthless, underappreciated, or maybe even incompetent. When you feel this way, your self-esteem plummets and your performance drops, neither of which contributes to being satisfied, valued, and fulfilled at work.

If your compensation is no longer aligned with the contributions you make in your organization, ask for a raise. Remember the employer-employee relationship is a social contract based on give-and-take. So you want to establish your request for a raise on your track record of exemplary performance. If your company has a formal review process, you have documentation of your performance. If not, schedule time with your manager to get feedback on your performance and share your goals. In the conversation, let your manager know that your priority is to excel in your current role and your long-term goal is to advance in your career. Solicit specific feedback on how you can improve in your current role and what you can do to prepare and position yourself for your next role.

As you implement your manager's feedback and continue to exceed expectations in your current position, proactively communicate your accomplishments. Your manager is busy and doesn't always know your achievements. When you talk to your manager, focus on the specific details of your successes and how they have positively impacted the business. For example:

- Did you increase revenue?
- Did you retain a client who was considering leaving?

- Did you receive positive feedback from a client, colleague, or leader in the organization regarding your work?

- Did you lead your team to find a solution to a challenging organizational problem?

- Was there a positive improvement/change as a result of your skills?

Emphasize how you've added value to your team and company. And don't forget to include the data. Numbers are observable and verifiable indicators of your performance. Consistently demonstrate your value in the organization and communicate it frequently.

You have solid performance. You've documented and consistently communicated your achievements to your manager. Now it's time to prepare to ask for a raise.

The first step is to do your research to determine your market value. When you ask for your raise, you want to know the salary ranges for professionals in your geographic area and in your industry with similar job titles, qualifications, and responsibilities. You can use sites like PayScale, Glassdoor, and Salary.com to find out the market rate for your current position or the position you want. If your manager asks you how much you'd like to make, be specific. For example, instead of saying you want $70,000 or $75,000, ask for $72,500. Researchers at Columbia Business School found that people appear more informed if they ask for a precise number.[6] Also, according to the Society for Human Resource Management, the average raise in 2020 will be 3.3 percent, up from 3.2 percent in 2019,[7] so keep this percentage in mind as you negotiate your raise (due to the Covid pandemic, this percentage may be lower than cited).

Your second preparation step is to write out and practice the conversation you want to have with your manager. In the discussion, summarize your accomplishments and their impact in the organization. It is important to focus on why you deserve the raise because of the value you've provided to the company and the quality of your work, versus why you need to make more money to pay your higher rent, take a vacation to the Caribbean, or host your friend's bachelorette party. And don't forget to communicate that you're invested in the future of the company. This offers a natural transition to what you want to do in the future and how you can contribute to grow the business.

Find a trusted colleague, friend, or partner and rehearse the conversation. Anticipate and practice answering questions your manager might ask. I've found that it is much easier to have a conversation that I think might be difficult or uncomfortable after role-playing it with a colleague or friend. When you schedule the meeting with your manager, let your manager know that the purpose of the meeting is to discuss your salary.

When the day of the meeting arrives, if the conversation goes well, and after some back-and-forth negotiations, you receive a raise, I want to share a huge congratulations! But I also want to address what happens if your manager says no. As my prior sales manager always told me, "No is just 'not now.'" A no from your manager does not have to be the end of the conversation and the negotiation. Ask for an interim performance review with clearly defined goals and a salary adjustment before your next annual review. Or if a raise or a promotion is not possible right now, get creative and ask for things beyond a salary increase like money to attend a professional development course or additional vacation days.

Financial compensation for your contributions at work is an important component of your engagement and fulfillment. If your compensation is not aligned to the impact you make in your organization, ask your manager to show you the money.

. . .

You are on a transformational journey to own, love, and make your job work for you. Acknowledge, identify, and ask for the recognition and appreciation you deserve in exchange for your contributions so you can turn any job into your dream job.

> Remember, I've created an Acceleration Guide on page 187 to support you on your transformational journey. You can also download a copy of it on my website www.carsontate.com/dreamjob.

CHAPTER FOUR

ALIGN YOUR STRENGTHS

Emma Herring left Colorado after graduating from law school and went to New York City to practice securities and business litigation for a global law firm.

"In my second year of law school, I decided I wanted to be a litigator. As an extern for a Colorado judge, I fell in love with the courtroom and the emotional highs and lows of a trial. So the opportunity to practice securities and business litigation for a global law firm in New York City was a dream come true for me," Emma said as we sat at an outside table eating our Chopt salads.

The days were long. Through the fog of sleep deprivation one Friday night while she struggled to catch up on all the missed deadlines on her case, Emma figured out a process to hold the law firm's team and the client's legal team accountable to ensure that all the case's deadlines were met. She immediately added project management to her legal responsibilities. "I'm very organized and proactive, and I like to get things done. Instead of writing the brief,

I wanted to make sure that the brief was written. Over the next eight months, I took on the project manager role in addition to my legal tasks on all my assigned cases. I loved it.

"Of course, then the doubts set in. Did I go to law school to manage deadlines?

"I wrestled for months with my doubts. When the litigation team almost missed a federal filing deadline for the firm's largest client, I saw that my project management strengths filled an essential need on our litigation team and that project management is a critical skill for practicing law. You need people like me to push people along to get things done. I learned to embrace it and not think of it as a lesser skill than the skill of the person that wrote the brief or deposed a witness. So I continued to do project management for my team in addition to my legal duties.

"However, after a year of working this way, I was still searching for a deeper purpose in my work. Deadlines were met. Our team won big, high-profile cases and made a lot of money. But I was not helping people in need. Then I met Susan, our law firm's full-time director of pro bono work. She helped me identify pro bono projects and nonprofits where I could use my litigation skills to make a significant, meaningful difference in people's lives. For example, I helped single moms expunge shoplifting from their criminal records so they could rent an apartment. Now I was using my legal skills in a way that mattered, had purpose, and truly changed people's lives for the better."

After five years in New York, Emma returned to Charlotte, North Carolina. The lifestyle of a litigator—all-nighters, Saturdays and Sundays spent at the office, and trials that could last months—did not align with how she wanted to raise her future family.

It was time for her to pivot in her career. Emma highlighted her project administration experience and strengths in the interview process. She accepted a position leading a law firm's legal project management program and its budget tracking. Under her leadership, Emma enhanced the firm's ability to manage legal matters efficiently, predictably, and profitably.

Emma made a fraction of what she had made as a corporate litigator. However, the lifestyle trade-off was worth it. She was home every night for dinner with her children, did not miss their soccer games on Saturday mornings, and started practicing yoga. Her personal life was rewarding, but there was a lack of fulfillment in her professional life. She began, like she had in New York, to question the meaning and value of her work.

Emma's law firm did not have a full-time pro bono director. She saw this as a tremendous opportunity not only for the firm, but for the community. She advocated to create the position at her law firm. Within a few months, she was named the firm's first Pro Bono Director. In this role, Emma brought together over 20 different legal departments and law firms to create an intentional model for pro bono service in Charlotte.

"I had to rely on my interpersonal skills, my ability to listen and understand to bring together people that are competitors. And going forward, I must use my project management strengths to make sure that things are actually getting done not for appearance purposes, but we are working on substantive projects that address the legal areas needed by low-income individuals in our community," she said.

Emma created her own path rather than follow those set before her to find both work-life balance and meaning in her work.

You are on a transformational journey to make your job align with your personal and professional needs and aspirations. To do this, don't *think* your way forward; *build* your way forward. As Emma did in her own career, when you build something, you try things; you experiment; you take calculated, thoughtful risks to determine what will ultimately work for you. This journey is not an existential journey. To turn any job into your dream job requires action, courage, and commitment to your dreams. Keep going. You can do this.

Your next step is to align your strengths to support the accomplishment of the company's goals so you can design your work in a way that meets both your professional and personal needs and goals.

STRENGTHS ARE
YOUR PROFESSIONAL GOLD

How often have you heard from a speaker at a conference, heard on a podcast, or read on a blog, "Play to your strengths" or "Leverage your strengths"? Your "strengths" are are the core of persistent, perennial strategy to enhance employee engagement. However, we often describe our strengths in vague terms. For example, I've lost count of the number of times I've told someone, "I'm good at getting things done." What does "good" mean? What exactly does "getting things done" look like? If you want to own, love, and make your job work for you, generic descriptions of your strengths will not work. It's time to get specific about your strengths so you can use them to achieve your company's goals and structure your work in a way that aligns with the life you want to live.

According to Marcus Buckingham, author of *Go Put Your Strengths to Work*, your strengths are the things you do consistently and near flawlessly. He asserts that there are four "SIGNs" of a strength—Success, Instinct, Growth, and Needs—and all four need to be considered when identifying a strength.[1]

Success indicates an activity that you have an ability in or how effective you feel at an activity.[2] For example, I have an ability to edit. I can read a document, and typos jump out at me like a neon flashing light. It's as if they scream at me, "Look at me; look at me." However, if I edit documents for more than a few hours a week, it's as though the life has been sucked out of me, and I want to crawl back in bed and hide under the covers. You will also have activities that are like this—all ability, but no desire. You can do these because you've got a natural gift for them, or because you're smart, or responsible, or diligent, but they bore you, drain you, or frustrate you. The strengths you want to focus on to be fulfilled and satisfied at work are more than the activities you are good at performing. Which is why there is a second aspect of a strength that is vital to consider: instinct.

When it comes to *instincts* and your strengths, you will feel an "I can't *not* do them" response to them.[3] You are instinctively, repeatedly drawn to these types of activities. Even though you might be fearful or anxious to do them, you find yourself wanting to do them though there is no rational reason. For example, when there is an opportunity to speak in front of people, my hand shoots into the air, almost on its own volition. I've been doing this since I was in Mrs. Risher's second grade class. However, as soon as my hand leaves my side and is above my head, sweat beads on my back, and my stomach clenches. What if I don't know what to say? What if I make a fool of myself? Despite the nervousness that arises every time I raise my hand, I still leap at every opportunity to speak in front of people. I can't help it. It's an instinct.

The third sign of a strength is *growth*. Growth refers to those activities that you are interested in, that you want to read about, study, and continue to refine with practice and new techniques.[4] Now these activities are not necessarily easy, but they challenge you in a way you *want* to be challenged. When you do these activities, you become immersed and you don't notice time passing. Why is this important? Because growth activities entice you to concentrate. Research by Mihaly Csikszentmihalyi, author of the book *Flow*, has shown that concentration and happiness are closely linked.[5] Happiness is a component of fulfillment, and fulfillment is one of your goals.

The final sign of a strength according to Buckingham is *needs*. "Whereas instinct refers to how you feel before you do the activity, and the growth signals to your feelings during the activity, the need sign points to how you feel after you have done it."[6] There are some activities that you do that fill innate needs of yours. You do them and may be tired, but you are not psychologically drained. You feel energized, joyful, powerful, engaged, and authentically yourself—the opposite of drained. It's that feeling of "all is right with the world."[7] It's a compelling feeling, and you need to feel it again. So, you seek out situations and opportunities where you can do this activity.

For example, my friend and colleague Gail is a trained coach. She will coach anyone, anywhere, at any time of day. At our favorite wine bar, she guided our regular waitress into her next career as a yoga instructor. Because she can't say no to an opportunity to coach, her assistant screens all her requests. When I have watched her coach our waiter, or the barista, or the flight attendant, she comes alive. Her eyes light up, and she smiles more. She becomes her most authentic, vibrant self. When we finally finish our meal or get our coffee or the flight lands, her energy is contagious.

When I asked Gail if she thought she would ever retire, she looked at me and said, "I feel most like me when I coach. I'd never give it up."

Your strengths are those activities that you are good at and you can't not do them. You seek out opportunities to develop them, and you need to do them. Your strengths make you feel strong, gratified, and fulfilled.

EXCAVATE YOUR STRENGTHS

When Emma decided to relocate from New York City, she knew that the lifestyle of a litigator did not align with how she would want to raise her future children. She decided to leverage her project management strengths to find a position as a project manager in a law firm so she would have more flexibility in her schedule. Your strengths are enablers of the life you want to lead. Strengths magnify your performance and potential. They can and will create opportunities for you to design your work in a way that meets both your professional and personal goals. When you use your strengths, you are more productive, impactful, and ultimately more fulfilled and engaged. Your strengths benefit your company *and* you. It is essential to know your strengths.

It is an excavation process to identify your strengths. When you excavate, you remove rocks and soil in order to find precious minerals, like gold. To find your gold, or your strengths, you will have to look below the surface of your day-to-day tasks. You will need to strip away generic descriptions to uncover the essence of your strengths. Three processes I use in my executive coaching practice to help my clients excavate their strengths are reflection journaling, performance reviews/360 feedback reports, and a calendar and task list analysis—all of which I will take you through in the coming pages.

It is vital that you complete either the reflection journaling, performance/360 review, or calendar and task list analysis process to identify your strengths. Why? Your strengths list is your employer relationship currency. It is what you offer your employer in exchange for more choice and control over how you work and what you work on. To effectively use your currency, you must know what it is *and* the value it provides to your employer. That is the potency of your strengths list. If you skip this process, it will be difficult to ask for and receive the projects and jobs that energize and excite you. It will also be difficult to shape your work in a way that aligns with the life you want to live. Don't give away your power, or your dreams. Invest the time and energy to excavate and identify your strengths.

Process #1: Reflection Journaling

Reflection journaling is a powerful tool for learning, growth, and change. It can help you identify important insights or key themes from experiences and events in your life. A reflection journal can provide a place for you to record and reflect upon your observations and responses to situations so you can analyze your patterns of thinking. It is also a place where you can get your ideas out of your head. I recommend reflection journaling to most of my coaching clients because of its effectiveness—and now, *you* are going to use it to identify your strengths.

Reflect on the following questions and record your answers on a piece of paper or in a document on your computer. Allot five to seven minutes a day for a week to answer these questions:

1. Think about your best day at work ever. What were you doing? (Hint: think about specific activities.)

2. When people praise you at work, what do they applaud?

3. What is the best compliment you've ever received at work? What made it the best?

4. I feel strong when . . .

5. I loved it today when I . . .

6. I can't help but to . . .

7. How would you describe your strengths?

At the end of the week, review your notes for any themes and patterns that emerged and use them to identify your strengths.

For example, if Emma had completed this exercise, she might have written that her best day at work was when she coordinated a group of attorneys to help pro bono clients expunge their arrest records after serving their sentences so that their legal record of an arrest or criminal conviction was "sealed," or erased in the eyes of the law. She would probably note that she receives frequent compliments on her project administration skills and her ability to unite people around a common goal. Emma might notice that she feels the strongest when she ensures that project deadlines are met for projects that support pro bono legal aid. Her notes might also reveal that she can't help but to connect people around important legal aid projects. As you reviewed Emma's answers, you likely saw a pattern: two of Emma's strengths are project management and exceptional interpersonal skills.

Review your notes to search for themes and patterns until you have identified at least three strengths. If you have more than three, don't worry. There is not a maximum number of strengths you can have.

Process #2: Performance Reviews/ 360 Feedback Reports

Performance reviews and 360 feedback reports provide data on instances when others observed consistent, near perfect performance from you, which is indicative of your strengths. However, it is important to remember that this is how *others* perceive your strengths, so you will still need to think about their feedback and then draft your own list of your strengths.

Use the steps below to identify your strengths based on others' feedback.

Step 1. Collect as many of your prior performance reviews and/or 360 feedback reports as possible. I typically ask clients to collect at least four total, and one should be your most recent performance review or 360 feedback report.

Step 2. As you read through your reviews and/or reports highlight or write down any statements that are made by at least four people. These statements indicate a pattern of consistent performance and illuminate a strength.

Step 3. Read through what you highlighted or wrote down and group the themes that emerged.

Step 4. Review the themes you grouped in the prior step and list what others observed as your strengths.

Step 5. Reflect on this list of strengths and modify or add any additional strengths that were not stated in your performance reviews or 360s.

If Emma were to review her 360s, she would probably note the following statements:

- "Emma is a very effective leader and team player. She delivers exemplary results and is caring, transparent, and ethical."

- "Emma executes plans with ease and holds people accountable. She has high integrity and is a trusted team player."

- "Emma expertly defines and plans projects and initiatives that support the firm's pro bono strategy."

- "Emma communicates clearly and inspires others to achieve goals. She deftly identifies the stakeholders, decision makers, and influencers required to achieve her goals and unites them to achieve her goals."

Emma would review the list of statements and identify her core theme as results oriented with strong execution, communication, and interpersonal expertise. She would then list her strengths as project administration and interpersonal abilities.

Process #3: Calendar and Task List Analysis

I might be biased; however, the calendar and task list analysis is my favorite method for my clients to identify their strengths. Why? Because this shows you, in black and white, how you spend your time and energy each day. As you examine your calendar and task list, you will be able to identify your strengths. And with this information, you will find opportunities to shift how you use your time so you can spend more time leveraging your strengths.

To identify your strengths, complete Steps 1 and 2 below at the end of each day for one workweek, which will take about 15 to 25 minutes. At the end of the workweek, complete the final three steps, which will take you between 20 and 45 minutes total.

Step 1. Review each meeting, appointment, and task you completed for the workday. Next to each meeting, appointment, and task, place a smiley face, plus sign, check mark, or up arrow next to anything you did that made you feel powerful, confident, natural, smooth, on fire, authentic, or awesome and/or made you say "That was easy" or "When do I get to do this again?" This step will help you identify the activities you love doing.

Step 2. Now, go back to the meetings, appointments, and tasks that you *did not* put a mark next to. If a task made you feel drained, bored, frustrated, irritated, or forced or made you think "Time is going so slowly" or "How much longer?," put a frowny face, minus sign, or down arrow. Your goal is to identify the activities you loathe doing. (We will come back to these when we explore how to design your work to meet your professional and personal goals.)

There will be some meetings, appointments, and tasks that are neutral because you neither love nor hate them. Leave them unmarked.

Step 3. At the end of the week, create a list of all the meetings, appointments, and tasks you loved doing. Then, rank them in order of what made you feel the most alive, engaged, authentic, and powerful.

Step 4. Take your list of ranked activities and select the top three activities. Then, ask yourself the questions below from Marcus Buckingham for each:

1. Does it matter *why* I do this activity?
2. Does it matter *whom* I do this activity with/to/for?
3. Does it matter *when* I do this activity?
4. Does it matter *what* this activity is about?[8]

When you ask yourself each of these four questions, you will discover exactly which aspects of this activity must be present for you to generate positive emotion. If you want to be engaged and fulfilled, you need to spend more time and energy on tasks that generate positive emotion. And you also want to design your work in a way that aligns with the way you want to live your life. Don't skip this vital step. Don't undermine your ability to ask for and work on the projects that invigorate you. Don't give away your power to ignorance of your strengths.

Now, let's look at an example of Step 4 in action. When I did my calendar and task list analysis, I put a smiley face next to the content analytics meeting with my team to decide on the next quarter's content marketing strategy.

1. Does it matter *why* I do this activity?

    Yes. I don't like reviewing analytics just to evaluate data. Analysis without a purpose feels like a waste of time to me. For this activity to produce positive emotions for me, it must be aligned to decision-making about our strategy or about prioritizing time, energy, and talent on the team.

2. Does it matter *whom* I do this activity with/to/for?

    No. I feel just as energized reviewing data with my team as I do when I review training and ROI data with my clients.

3. Does it matter *when* I do this activity?

    Yes and no. I'm a morning person and do my best thinking early in the day. My energy drops midafternoon, and I'm not as effective, nor am I as efficient, with cognitively demanding tasks or with decision-making.

4. Does it matter *what* this activity is about?

    Yes. I'm demotivated and drained when I prepare and analyze data that is not connected to a broader strategy, goal, or purpose.

These questions also help you write a description of your strengths that is specific enough that you can clearly articulate to yourself, your manager, and your organization how your strengths enable the organization to achieve its goals. It is imperative that you demonstrate how your strengths add value to the organization so you can spend more time using them.

> **Step 5.** Narrow down your list to your top three strengths, and for each, fill in the following strengths statement: "My strength is _____."

After reviewing my own answers in Step 4, I wrote the description of my strength as "Analyze data to make decisions about strategic goals and internal resource allocations and priorities."

Remember, your goal is identify exactly which aspects of the activity are critical for you to be able generate the same positive emotions each and every time you perform it. Specificity is essential.

• • •

Congratulations! You have identified your strengths! How do you feel? When my clients identify their strengths, their eyes light up, the tension in their shoulders abates, and I can feel a shift in their energy. They feel more powerful, energized, and confident. These are just some of the emotions you experience when you are engaged, fulfilled, and happy at work—which is what you want more of in your professional life. So, let's put your strengths to work for your organization so you can spend more time energized, impactful, and engaged.

LEVERAGE YOUR STRENGTHS FOR MORE CHOICE AND CONTROL OVER YOUR WORK

In order to put your strengths to work for your organization, it is first important to remember that the employer-employee relationship is a social contract based on give-and-take. When you can use your strengths to enable your company to achieve its strategic goals, generate revenue, and/or serve clients, you provide value and give to the relationship. This puts you in a powerful and mutually beneficial place to then receive from the relationship or make an ask of your employer.

Emma asked her New York law firm to pay for her to get her project management professional certification and to put her on the highest-profile cases with the largest global clients. When she moved to Charlotte, she asked her firm for flexible work hours and now works from home on Fridays. Emma also leveraged her strengths to create a position for herself as her firm's pro bono administrator.

Do not underestimate your value and your power when you choose to employ your strengths in your relationship with your employer. Use the four steps below to align your strengths to your company's and team's goals so you can have more choice and control over what you work on and how you work.

Align Your Strengths to Your Organization's Goals

It will take you approximately 30 minutes to complete the following four steps:

Step 1: Ensure that you are clear on your company's and team's current goals. Review the company's strategic plan and your team's goals.

Step 2: For each of your company's and team's goals, identify how your top three strengths support the attainment of any, all, or some of the goals. Your objective is to draw a distinct and clear line between your strengths and the successful attainment of your company's and team's goals. Be specific and use the following questions to help connect your strengths to your company's and team's success:

1. How can your company and/or team achieve its goals faster when you leverage your strengths?

2. How can your company and/or team achieve its goals more profitably when you use your strengths?

3. How can your company and/or team be more productive when you leverage your strengths?

4. How do your strengths contribute to innovation or new product development?

5. How do your strengths enable your company to more effectively serve its customers ? This could be through automation, higher customer satisfaction scores, or faster problem or complaint resolution.

6. How do your strengths enable the company to differentiate itself from its competitors?

Step 3: Review your past projects. For each project, explore how you leveraged your strengths to effectively achieve the project goal. Review the questions above to help you draw a distinct and clear line between your strengths and the successful accomplishment of the company's and team's goals. The objectives in this step are to demonstrate a track record of efficacious alignment between your strengths and the company's and team's goals and to catalog your goals achieved.

Step 4: Brainstorm additional ways you can deploy your strengths to support your company's and team's goals. When you use your strengths, can the goal be achieved faster? More effectively? Less expensively? Or more profitably? Again, identify the specific projects and tasks that you can do more of so you can work from your strengths more often. Your goal is to demonstrate that when you work from your strengths, your company and team benefit.

You now have a clear picture of how your strengths have enabled your team and company to achieve their goals. But what about those tasks and activities that aren't your strengths, or that you detest doing? You want to be engaged and fulfilled at work, and time spent on activities that you despise will not help make that a reality. So how can you spend less time on those activities? Use the three steps below to stop, reduce, partner, or reframe the activities you loathe doing. It will take you approximately 20 minutes to complete these steps, and your goal is to do less of these activities you loathe and do more of those activities you love.

Stop, Reduce, Partner, or Reframe Activities You Loathe Doing

Step 1: Review the items you marked with a frowny face, a minus sign, or a down arrow in your calendar and task list analysis. These are the appointments, meetings, and tasks that you loathe doing. If you did not select this option to identify your strengths, go back and complete Step 2 in the calendar and task list analysis so you can identify the activities you loathe doing.

Step 2: Put the activities that you loathe doing on one of four lists—stop, reduce, partner, reframe.

- **Stop.** Write down on the "stop" list all the activities that are not critical to your success in your job and/or that no one would notice if you no longer completed. Beside each one, identify whom you need to talk to in your company to make this a reality. There may be activities that you don't need to talk to anyone about—you can just stop doing them.

- **Reduce.** Write down on your "reduce list" all the activities that you can't stop doing but that you could reduce the time you spend on them. For each activity on the reduce list, ask yourself if there is a way to automate it. If you can't automate it, then time yourself to see how long it takes and then try to beat your time.

- **Partner.** Write down all the activities that you could partner with someone to either trade with a colleague or make the activity faster or more fun. For example, you would do an activity that a colleague does not like, and your colleague would do one you don't like. If you can't think of anyone to swap the activity with, think about who might be able to teach you a new technique or strategy to do it faster. Or consider who in your office would make doing this activity more fun and beneficial if you did it together.

- **Reframe.** The reality is that there are going to be some activities that you can't stop doing, that you can't reduce the amount of time you spend on them, and that don't match up with a colleague's strengths. For these activities you need to reframe.

  To reframe and reduce the negative impact of this activity, consider alternating a strength activity with an activity that drains you, or change the time when you complete the activity. If you normally complete this task in the afternoon or on a specific day, maybe try doing it in the morning or on a different day when your energy is higher. Also consider how you can shift your perspective so that you can see this activity as just one step of many that lead to the successful accomplishment of your goal.

Step 3: Once you have your four lists completed, act on each one. If you need to talk to someone to stop doing an activity, schedule the meeting now. If you don't need to talk to someone, stop doing that activity today. If you need to explore your options for how to automate and reduce the time you spend on activities that drain you, start the process.

See whom you can partner up with to swap tasks, learn how to complete the activity faster, or just make completing it more fun. And don't forget, you can always reframe and shift your perspective so you can see how this activity moves you one step closer to your goal.

Don't Let Fear Undermine Your Power

Strengths enable you to have more control over what you work on and how you work. In exchange for using your strengths to help your company and team achieve their goals, what do you want from the relationship with your employer? If you are not clear on what you want and need from your employer, how could your employer ever provide it? Now at this point, I imagine a few doubts have crept in. You might be thinking, "You don't know my boss. She would never agree to pay for additional training or allow me to work from home on Fridays. You want me to create a role in the company that does not exist? She wouldn't even *consider* that." I understand your reservations. However, when I have doubts and fears about my ability to ask for what I need, I hear David Clay, my former sales manager at Bristol-Myers Squibb, saying, "If you don't ask, you will not receive." You have to ask. Otherwise you operate from assumptions and remain unclear about the real possibilities that may exist for you.

Fear undermines your power. Focus on what you want more of in your professional life, how this will catapult your career, and how this ask will benefit your family, your partner, and/or your community. You will not know what is possible if you do not ask. You can do this. Feel the fear and do it anyway.

Be Bold and Ask for What You Want

At this point, you have now identified how your strengths support and enable your company to achieve its goals, and you've learned how to stop, reduce, reframe, or partner on the activities you loathe so you can spend more time working from your strengths. Now that you have all this information, you need to meet with your manager and specifically ask for what you want and need to meet your professional and personal goals.

Remember that your strengths are your contributions to the employer-employee relationship and the value you provide. Your strengths are your professional gold. If you need to discuss an activity that you want to stop doing, include it on your agenda for your manager. Be bold and ask for the changes you want so you have more control and choice over what you work on and how you work.

. . .

"I want to go work every day and not question the sacrifice I'm making as a working mom. My job matters. I am doing something I believe in and using my strengths. My life has purpose," Emma told me. Her clarity around her strengths enabled her to hone them and then leverage them to build a career and a life so she could achieve both her professional and personal goals. Emma consistently aligned her strengths to the needs and goals of the organization and used this alignment to ultimately create a position that did not exist in her law firm in Charlotte.

Again, strengths amplify performance. In 2018 Emma received the 2018 Distinguished Pro Bono Service Award, a lifetime achievement honor presented by the Charlotte Center for Legal

Advocacy, the Council for Children's Rights, and Legal Aid of North Carolina. Strengths enable the life you want to lead. Emma currently cochairs Parent Education at her children's school, and, fortunately for me, she frequently joins me for girls' night out. Strengths are your professional gold.

STEP TWO

LOVE IT.

REKINDLE PASSION AND JOY IN YOUR WORK

DEVELOP new skills and knowledge

CULTIVATE authentic relationships

YOUR DREAM JOB

| ADMIT | ALIGN | DEVELOP | CULTIVATE | DESIGN |

YOUR SKILLS + EXPERIENCES + VALUES

CHAPTER FIVE

DEVELOP NEW SKILLS AND KNOWLEDGE

As Chloe walked into our local wine bar, there was a sparkle in her eyes and a huge smile on her face. Well rested from her week in Arizona over spring break and just back from a trip to New York with the CEO of the company where she has worked for 20 years, she was energized and excited when she sat down at our favorite high-top table. As a managing partner at one of the largest financial services firms, back-to-back meetings, numerous deadlines, a full to-do list, and high stress were part of her job description. However, I rarely heard Chloe complain about her work, and she appeared happy, engaged, and professionally fulfilled.

After our glasses of sauvignon blanc and our bowl of roasted nuts arrived, I jumped right in. "I've been spending a lot of time with clients who are unhappy, demotivated, and unfulfilled at work. And I'm meeting more and more people across the country who dread Monday mornings. This does not appear to be you. How do you do it? What is your secret?"

Chloe said, "I think it's a combination of a few things, actually. From an early age I was fascinated by business. At 15, I was reading *Fortune*, *Forbes*, and *BusinessWeek*."

Chloe gave me a smile, perhaps because she knew me well enough to know that at 15 I was reading *Cosmo* and *Seventeen* and trying to learn how to apply my blue eye shadow so it accented my green eyes. It took me a little bit longer to find my passion.

"I was interested in global financial markets. I was good at math and analyzing data. So when I went to college, I majored in finance," Chloe added.

"Why did you choose to work for the bank?"

"Well, I chose the bank because it was global, and I could have 20 different careers within one company. This was intriguing to me," she said. "Our industry is changing so rapidly, I have to continue to develop new expertise to stay current. You know I love to learn!"

Chloe continued. "Did you know that I've never applied for a job since I applied the first time?"

"Really? That's incredible!"

"Every time I've accepted a new job it was because someone called me and said I want you to join our group. Why? Because I volunteered for other initiatives in the bank which allowed me to interact with people I would not normally interact with. I built a reputation for achieving results, synthesizing the complex, and successfully navigating a complex organization."

A few key themes emerged for me as Chloe continued to talk. First, choose an industry that interests you. Second, know your strengths and leverage those strengths in your work. Third, develop yourself. And finally, build relationships and connections throughout your company.

Each of these is an essential step on your transformational journey to love your work and turn any job into your dream job. You've already unleashed your superpowers of choice and control, acknowledged your appreciation and recognition needs, and identified your strengths and used them to shape your work in a way that meets both your professional and personal needs and goals. Now let's follow in Chloe's footsteps and take the next step: develop yourself. This requires that you acquire new capabilities and knowledge and find ways to advance in your career. You chose to invest in yourself, and it's an investment that pays off—in increased confidence, additional opportunities for a promotion or a raise, enhanced value to your team and company, and more time and energy for the people, hobbies, and projects that interest you. Professional growth and development enable you to stay agile, excited, passionate, and engaged in your job. Assess your current skills and knowledge to create your own professional development plan.

CREATE YOUR ABILITIES OPPORTUNITY MAP

To develop new capabilities and expertise, you need to assess your current skills. This following process will help you easily identify your ability gaps and the new competencies and experiences you need to be enthusiastic and content in your work.

Let's create your Abilities Opportunity Map. It is a chart of the aptitudes and capabilities you want to cultivate. To download a blank Abilities Opportunity Map, go to www.carsontate.com/dreamjob. (There is also a blank Abilities Opportunity Map in Appendix 2 in the back of this book.)

Step 1. Assess Your Current Skills

The first step in this process is to assess your current skills. Read each statement below and check if the statement is true or false for you.

	TRUE	FALSE
In my last performance review, my manager recommended that I develop new skills and/or attend a specific training or certification program.		
I was passed over for a promotion because I lacked specific skills or knowledge.		
I do not have the skills to qualify for another position if my job was eliminated.		
I struggle to complete projects because I lack the knowledge and skills.		
Most of my teammates have some skills, or certifications, that I do not have.		
I sometimes must ask my teammates to show me how to perform tasks in my job.		
I decided not to get certified or recertified in my job. (Only answer if your job involves certifications.)		
I believe I am "stagnating" or "not going anywhere" at work.		
I could provide better services to our customers if I had more skills.		
My company has a defined set of leadership abilities and aptitudes, and I don't have all of them.		

Review the questions that you marked true. These highlight where you need to focus your attention to identify the specific skill set you need and want to develop in your job. This is *not* a list of your inadequacies, imperfections, or failings. Each true statement is a place on your Abilities Opportunity Map that you choose to visit, explore, and learn more about. These true statements can be considered a "skill set destination" on your professional development journey.

If you're like most of my clients, you probably have heard the term "skill set" so often you haven't really thought about what it actually means in quite a while. I think it's important to revisit the meaning. A skill set is a collection of abilities, qualities, and experiences you have and can apply.

There are three types of skill sets: soft skills, hard skills, and hybrid skills.

- **Soft skills** are interpersonal abilities you use to interact with other people. For example, communication, listening, empathy, agility, and teamwork. These skills are transferable and valuable in any job in any industry.

- **Hard skills** are technical capabilities you use to perform a task related to a specific job. For example, accounting, data analysis, SEO marketing, information technology, or copywriting.

- **Hybrid skills** are a combination of both soft and hard skills. For example, a customer service representative would need the soft skills of exceptional communication and conflict resolution expertise, as well as the hard skill of proficiency with a customer relationship management software program.

Step 2. Identify the Specific Skills and Expertise You Want to Develop

The second step to construct your Abilities Opportunity Map is to identify and clarify the specific skills and expertise you want and need to develop. This is a critical step. Each aptitude you distinguish is a destination on your Abilities Opportunity Map. It is *where* you want to go on the journey to develop yourself.

Below you will see all the questions from Step 1. For any that you marked true, answer the corresponding prompts that begin on page 97. This exercise will take you between 30 and 45 minutes to complete. You are worth the time. This is an investment in your professional development, growth, career, and future.

Now, a few of the prompts are basic and probably obvious. This is intentional. It will help you synthesize and organize your thoughts and data. You need specific information to determine exactly what aptitudes and expertise you want to develop. And your answers to the questions will also guide *how* you will acquire your new skills.

As you answer each of the prompts for each question you marked true, do not worry about the form or structure of your notes and reflections. The objective in this step is simply to collect information. In Step 3 you will review your notes and organize them.

Question 1	Prompts
In my last performance review, my manager recommended that I develop new skills and/ or attend a specific training or certification program.	Review your most recent performance review. • What specific skill or skills did your manager recommend? • What specific certification program did your manager recommend?
Question 2	**Prompts**
I was passed over for a promotion because I lacked specific skills or knowledge.	Compare your current résumé with the job description for the position you did not receive. • What skills listed on the job description do you not have? • What qualifications listed on the job description do you not have? • What certifications or credentials listed on the job description do you not have? • What experiences listed on the job description do you not have? • What skills listed on the job description have you recently acquired that need to be further developed? • If you know the person who was hired for the position, what skills, qualifications, certifications, and/or experiences does this person have that you do not have? • If you don't know the person, how might you find out the skills, qualifications, certifications, and/or experiences that the person has that you do not have?

(continued on the next page)

Question 3	Prompts
I do not have the skills to qualify for another position if my job was eliminated.	• Is your current skill set highly technical or very niched? • Does your company have a list of capabilities or core competencies required for a leadership position within the company? If so, compare your current skill set with the list of the leadership core competencies to identify capability gaps.
Question 4	**Prompts**
I struggle to complete projects because I lack the knowledge and skills.	Review your to-do list and/or your list of current projects to help you answer the questions below: • What project did you struggle to complete because you lacked the knowledge? • What specific knowledge was required to complete this project? • What project did you find difficult to complete because you lacked the skills? • What specific skills were required to complete this project?
Question 5	**Prompts**
Most of my teammates have some skills, or certifications, that I do not have.	• What are the skills your teammates have that you do not have? • What are the certifications your teammates have that you do not have?
Question 6	**Prompts**
I sometimes must ask my teammates to show me how to perform tasks in my job.	Review your to-do list and/or job description to help you answer the questions below: • What task(s) did you ask a teammate for help with? • What teammate did you ask for help? • What criteria did you use to determine which person to ask for help? • What are the person's aptitudes? Talents? Abilities? Knowledge?

Question 7	Prompts
I decided not to get certified or recertified in my job. (*Only* answer if your job involves certifications.)	• Why did you choose not to get certified or recertified? • What certifications are available for your profession? For example, a certification that is available for project managers is the Project Management Professional designation. A quick Google search can help you identify the certifications available in your profession. • What specific certification did you choose not to obtain? • What specific certification did you choose not to recertify?

Question 8	Prompts
I believe I am "stagnating" or "not going anywhere" at work.	• Is there an opportunity to advance or be promoted in your job? For example, if you are currently a customer support specialist, is there a customer support specialist two position in your company? • Look at the job description for this position. What are the capabilities, experiences, and qualifications needed for this role? • If there is not an opportunity to advance in your job, is there another job that interests you? • Look at the job description for this position. What are the capabilities, experiences, and qualifications needed for this role? • Is it possible that you don't find meaning, value, and purpose in your job? When my executive coaching clients say yes to this question and have the same insight you just had, we shift gears and toolboxes. As is true for my clients, you are on a different path, and you need a different set of tools. Meaning, value, and purpose are not skill sets. These are how you relate to and experience your work. The job of your dreams is waiting, so please stop reading this chapter now and go to Chapter Seven to find the tools you need to design your job to find your meaning.

(continued on the next page)

Question 9	Prompts
I could provide better services to our customers if I had more skills.	• What does "better services" look like? For example, resolve customers' complaints while on the phone with them. You don't have to call them back because you know how to fix the top five challenges your customers face when they try to install your software. • Based on your definition of "better services," what skill or skills do you want to develop? • Who on your team has the highest customer service scores? • What does that person do when interacting with customers that you do not do when you interact with your customers? • What specific skills does the person have that you do not have?

Question 10	Prompts
My company has a defined set of leadership competencies, and I don't have all of them.	It can be helpful to look at your last performance review if it lists your company's leadership competencies. Or if the leadership competencies are new or you don't have a formal performance review, go to your company's website and download them, or ask your human resources department or your manager for a copy of them. • What data do you have that indicates you do not possess all the leadership competencies? • Were you given this feedback by your manager? • Was it on your performance review? • Did a mentor or trusted colleague provide this insight? List your current leadership competencies. You may need to have a conversation with a colleague, a mentor, or your manager to help you clearly recognize them. Compare your list with the company's leadership competencies and identify the ones you do not possess.

You now have copious notes and data on the specific aptitudes and expertise you want to develop. Take a moment and acknowledge yourself for your commitment to yourself and your professional development. Completing Step 2 is a significant, powerful step. Well done!

If you are like my clients, you may feel overwhelmed right now. I get it. You have pages of notes, data, and documentation, and you may be thinking to yourself, "What am I going to do with all this information?" The answer is it's time to organize your answers to each prompt by the type of skill set you need to develop to acquire your new knowledge or expertise. Let's move on to Step 3.

Step 3. Identify the Type of Skill Set You Need to Develop

The third step to build your Abilities Opportunity Map is to identify the type of skill set you need to develop. This is an essential step because it will inform *how* you will acquire the skill set. On a piece of paper, or on your computer, draw three columns. At the top of the first column write "Soft Skills." Above the second column write "Hard Skills," and above the third column write "Hybrid Skills."

Soft Skills	Hard Skills	Hybrid Skills

Then return to Step 2 and review your answers to the prompts for each question you marked "true." As you review each response, write it in either the Soft Skills, Hard Skills, or Hybrid Skills column. An example is included below:

Soft Skills	Hard Skills	Hybrid Skills
• Refine my presentation skills to be more succinct, direct, and to the point • Develop my ability to communicate a compelling vision for the team • Enhance my ability to build support within the company for my team's initiatives and navigate the corporate hierarchy • Learn how to lead an organization-wide change management initiative and anticipate and adjust to challenges as needed • Increase innovation skills to develop creative, effective solutions to business problems • Develop increased awareness and understanding of the challenges associated with doing business internationally and the different business practices required for success	• Learn advanced Excel pivot tables to analyze competitor market capitalization • Learn Outlook rules to reduce time spent processing email	• Refine my ability to communicate succinctly and consistently using the tools in Outlook

Step 4. Prioritize the Top Three Skills You Want to Develop

You've probably heard the Lao-tzu saying, "A journey of 1,000 miles begins with a single step." This is true for you right now. You have a list of numerous soft, hard, and hybrid skills that you want to develop. The reality is that you can't do them all right now. However, you are committed to your professional development and advancing your career. Let's prioritize the top three skills you want to develop in the next 6 to 12 months. Review your list of soft, hard, and hybrid skills and select the three that will enable you to make a significant impact quickly, are directly tied to a professional goal or objective, and/or enable you to distinguish yourself on your team and within your company.

An example is below:

My Top Three Skills to Develop

Skills to Develop	Skill Type
1. Refine my presentation skills to be more succinct, direct, and to the point	Soft
2. Enhance my ability to build support within the company for my team's initiatives and navigate the corporate hierarchy	Soft
3. Learn how to lead an organization-wide change management initiative and anticipate and adjust to challenges as needed	Soft

Your Abilities Opportunity Map is almost complete! So far, you have (1) assessed your current skills, (2) identified the specific capabilities and aptitudes you want and need to develop, (3) organized your specific competencies and expertise by type of skill set—soft skill, hard skill, or hybrid skill—and (4) prioritized the top three skills you want to develop. Great work! You have just one final step to complete your map—determine how to acquire your new skills or knowledge.

Step 5. Determine How to Acquire Your New Skills and Knowledge

For each one of your top three skills you chose to develop, determine and write down how you will acquire that new capability or knowledge. You may decide that you want or need to combine one or two of the options to acquire your new skills. That's fine. This is your professional development plan.

You will need to have your Abilities Opportunity Map next to you as you read the following section.

SKILL DEVELOPMENT OPTIONS

In this section, you will see your development options grouped by skill set: soft skills, hard skills, and hybrid skills. As you read each option, decide if it will enable you to acquire one of your top three skills. If it will, write that option next to the skill in the "How?" column of your Abilities Opportunity Map.

Soft Skill Acquisition Options

Remember, soft skills are interpersonal abilities you use to interact with other people. For example, communication, listening, empathy, agility, and teamwork. Below are some ways that you can acquire soft skills.

Get a Coach

Coaching is an action-oriented, goal-focused process to improve performance, guide self-discovery, and make behavioral shifts. It is future-focused and believes that the individual being coached has the capacity for positive self-actualization.

This is one of the most effective ways to develop soft skills. You work one-on-one with a coach, so you have a safe, nonjudgmental place to practice and receive feedback on the skill(s) you want to develop. This is essential because soft skills, such as active listening or conflict resolution, require a consistent practice-feedback-practice loop to learn. You and your coach meet regularly, which helps you stay accountable and committed to applying your new skills.

Your company may have internal coaches or a relationship with a coaching firm. Contact your human resources department to find a coach at your company. Or you can find an external coach through the International Coach Federation. This is a global organization with over 25,000 professionally trained coaches. On its website, you can search for a coach based on location and/or the specific skill set you want to obtain or improve. We also have a team of certified coaches trained in the strategies and tools in this book.*

Mentoring

Mentoring can be either a formal or an informal learning relationship. A mentor can share technical information, institutional knowledge, insights into your company's culture or politics, or broad insights about leadership, networking, communication, and teamwork.

Find and develop a relationship with a person who has been in your shoes, is where you want to be in your career, and is willing to give you unvarnished, honest feedback. For example, one of my coaching clients is Jade, a minority female physician in a large healthcare system. She developed a mentoring relationship with another minority female, Prisha, who understood the hospital's politics, had successfully navigated the patriarchal, white-male culture of the system, and had two high-profile leadership positions in the system. Jade asked for her mentorship so she could refine her own leadership skills and understand how to acquire leadership positions in the healthcare system.

A mentoring relationship is more dynamic and fluid than coaching. You may or may not meet regularly with your mentor.

---

* Sometimes it is easier to do this work with the help of a coach. If you'd like to meet with one of the Working Simply certified coaches to help you own, love, and make your job work for you, visit www.carsontate.com/coaching to learn more.

And if you want feedback from your mentor on your soft skills, your mentor must have opportunities to see you use them.

Check with your company's human resources department to find out if it has a formal mentoring program and, if so, how to get involved. If your company does not have a formal mentoring program, identify the person, as Jade did, who demonstrates the knowledge, skills, or expertise you want to obtain and reach out to that person.

Training Courses

A training course can be an in-person class, a virtual instructor-led class such as a webinar, a self-paced online module, or a combination of these three.

A training curriculum will help you develop soft skills; it is designed to teach you the mechanics of soft skills. For example, in a communications training course you may learn to restate what you heard to show you were actively listening and to enable others to clarify what they said if you've misheard or misunderstood them.

It is important to think about how you will practice and receive feedback on the skill(s) you learn in a training class. Depending on the type of program, you may have the opportunity to practice in the class and receive feedback from the instructor. However, to change your current behavior and develop new behavior requires consistent practice and feedback. Solicit your manager, teammates, and/or peers to give you feedback when you practice your new skill(s) in a setting where they can watch you, such as a meeting. Ask them to observe your behavior and then provide feedback immediately after the event. For additional tips on how to ask for feedback, go to page 45.

Now let's explore the options you have to acquire hard skills.

Hard Skills Acquisition Options

Hard skills are technical capabilities you use to perform a task related to a specific job—for example, accounting, data analysis, SEO marketing, information technology, or copywriting. Below are some ways that you can acquire hard skills.

Training Courses

Training courses are an exceptional way to learn new technical skills. Trainings typically target a specific hard skill or set of hard skills, such as how to use Excel pivot tables or how to use technology to manage your email. For example, you could attend one of our Tame Your Inbox trainings to learn how to write rules, create custom templates, and color-code incoming messages from your manager.* You can find a training curriculum for the specific capabilities you want to develop through your company's human resources department, through your professional association, by attending conferences, or on the Internet.

Job Shadowing

When you job-shadow, you work with and observe another employee who has demonstrated expertise in the skills, behaviors, and/or competencies you want to acquire. It can involve hands-on training, observation, or a combination of both. You can shadow a person for a few hours, days, or even weeks, depending on the type of skill and knowledge you want to develop. To find a job

---

* My company, Working Simply, offers training programs designed to help you develop the soft, hard, and hybrid skills you need to achieve your career goals and enjoy an engaged and fulfilled work life. Visit www.workingsimply.com to learn more.

shadowing opportunity, talk to your manager and/or your human resources department to identify the best person for you to shadow.

Lastly, let's look at the options you have to acquire hybrid skills.

Hybrid Skills Acquisition Options

Since hybrid skills are a combination of both soft and hard competencies, the first step is to use the development options listed above to identify your best option. Three additional routes can be helpful to identify the proficiencies you may need to advance in your career and how you can obtain them.

Informational Interview

In this type of discussion, you seek out and talk to coworkers, thought leaders, and/or industry experts who have the specific job, career, and/or aptitudes you want to obtain. The objective of the conversation is to understand *how* they achieved success and got to where they are today. Before you meet with someone, do your research so you can ask specific questions that will support your own professional development.

Below are essential questions to ask to understand how the person you selected to interview achieved success. However, you might find the answers to some of the questions as you complete your interview preparation. Add and remove questions from this list based on your research and your own professional development goals.

- What are one or two things you wish you had known when you started in this profession?

- What, if anything, would you do differently?

- What, if anything, would you do the same way?

- What are the challenges or setbacks you have experienced in your career? How did you overcome them?

- What skills do you use regularly?

- How did you acquire these skills?

- What capability are you currently developing? What prompted you to focus on developing this now?

- Are there any books, magazines, trade publications, websites, or podcasts you recommend?

Peer Relationships

Relationships with people in your industry are essential. These associations enable you to stay current on industry trends, certifications, and competencies and to gain new perspectives and ideas. You can foster connections with people in your industry through networking at conferences, professional association or trade events, or local business events.

Once you develop peer relationships, it is important to nurture them. These relationships are about give-and-take, so remember to proactively add value and support your peers. Proactively reach out to your network and ask questions for advice and feedback to help you advance your career.

Experiential Assignments and Opportunities

Real-life experiences are one of the most powerful and fastest ways to learn and develop new knowledge and competencies. There are two primary ways you can engage in an experience: participate in a task force or take part in action learning. A task force is a group of people who work on a specific project. A task force may also be called a committee or a special project team and typically includes people from different divisions within a company. Action learning is a *process* that involves a group of people who work on a real and important challenge to the organization, solve that problem by practicing new skills, and then reflect on the experience in order to learn and grow from the experience.

Either of these opportunities enables you to practice new skills and observe others in real situations. You can observe how others lead through conflict, how they make decisions, how they navigate company politics and achieve goals. To find a task force or an action learning opportunity, talk to your manager, your human resources department, or your mentor. You may also have the opportunity to participate in action learning if you are part of a leadership development program at your company.

Congratulations! Your Abilities Opportunity Map is complete!

An example of a completed Abilities Opportunity Map is below:

My Top Three Skills to Develop

Skills to Develop	Skill Type	How?
1. Refine my presentation skills to be more succinct, direct, and to the point	Soft	Training class
2. Enhance my ability to build support within the company for my team's initiatives and navigate the corporate hierarchy	Soft	Informational interview and mentoring
3. Learn how to lead an organization-wide change management initiative and anticipate and adjust to challenges as needed	Soft	Coaching

CREATE YOUR PROFESSIONAL DEVELOPMENT PLAN

Now that you have your own Abilities Opportunity Map, you need to select the specific coach, mentor, training program, job shadowing opportunity, informational interview, peer networking opportunity, and/or experience that will enable you to acquire each of your top three development skills. There are a vast variety of professional development options available to you. It can be overwhelming. To narrow down the plethora of options, you will use three words to guide the assessment and selection process— *equip*, *empower*, and *inspire*. These three words make up the mission statement for my company, Working Simply. It is the essence of what we do and how we best serve our clients. And I'd like to suggest you use the same words to serve yourself.

The approach you will use below will help you assess the immense array of available professional development options so you can select the best one for you. This approach has been field-tested and proved with our clients and all our internal training, consulting, and coaching programs.

Start with the first skill you want to develop and how you decided to acquire it. For example, the first skill on the example Abilities Opportunity Map is "Refine my presentation skills to be more succinct, direct, and to the point." You decided to develop this skill through training. As you review the presentation skills training options you found on the Internet, on your company's learning management system, or on your professional association's website, ask yourself the questions beneath "Equip," "Empower," and "Inspire" below for each of the three skills you have chosen to develop. (Some of the questions refer specifically to coaching or training. If this is not an option you are evaluating, skip those questions. Or if there is a question that does not apply to the skill acquisition methodology you selected, skip it.)

Equip:

- Will this _____ equip me with the skills I want and need for my professional development and growth?
- What specific skills does the training course teach?
- What are the learning objectives for the training course?
- What is the coach's area of expertise and experience?
- Is this person proficient in the use of the skills I want to acquire? Does this person have a demonstrated track record of success?

Empower:

- Will this _____ empower me and prepare me to apply and integrate my new capabilities and expertise into my workday, life, and/or career?
- What job aid or quick reference guides are provided in the training class?
- What case studies are used to illustrate how to apply the concepts taught in the training curriculum?
- What opportunities do I have to practice and apply the skill during this _____?
- How does this _____ prepare me for the challenges I will encounter when I apply and integrate this new skill into my workday, life, and/or career?

Inspire:

- How will this _____ motivate and inspire me when I hit a challenge or roadblock when I apply my new skills?

- What tools and strategies does this _____ include to help me develop new, sustainable habits?

- What ongoing support does this _____ provide?

There is no one-size-fits-all nor "right" or "wrong" professional development program. Select the plan and/or people who will equip, empower, and inspire you so you can turn any job into your dream job.

• • •

As Chloe and I neared the end of our glasses of wine, I asked her a question I thought I knew the answer to, but I wanted to write her answer down in her own words.

"What is your most significant professional accomplishment?" I asked.

Smiling broadly, Chloe told me, "As you probably guessed, my most significant professional accomplishment ocurred within the last year. After 18 years as the CFO of various business lines within the bank, I now lead our global banking and digital strategy division. I'm on the front line, and my global responsibilities generate more than one billion in annual revenue."

"You have watched me through the years learn new skills," she continued. "Remember when I transitioned into mobile banking and had never worked in technology? And how I had to take the monthlong training class on our mobile banking software? That was a *very* long month. And remember when I went to Switzerland and presented on credit risk after identifying I could use this knowledge to help the bank build its brand as a thought leader in credit risk mitigation?"

"Oh yes! I remember both of those! I am very proud of you and all that you have accomplished in your career," I said.

We drank our last sip of wine, paid the bill, and walked out to our cars.

You can feel about your career the way Chloe feels about hers. You are ready to develop new skills and knowledge and advance your career so you can turn any job into your dream job. If I gave you a magic wand that transported you into the future and asked you the same question I asked Chloe—"What is your most significant professional accomplishment?"—what would you tell me? Use your Abilities Opportunity Map to make your goals and dreams a reality.

CHAPTER SIX

CULTIVATE AUTHENTIC RELATIONSHIPS

Do any of these complaints sound familiar?

"Why does she always wait until the absolute last minute to complete her tasks? Because of her, the entire office always seems to spend the final day of any project frantically rushing around to meet the deadline! It's too stressful. I won't work on her team again."

"Every email I receive from him is a sentence or less— sometimes just a few letters. The last email he sent me read 'K TX.' What the heck does that mean!? Why can't he communicate in full sentences and treat me like a human being, not a robot."

"I like my manager, but every time I visit her with a quick question, we must discuss her weekend and her three children's latest incredible accomplishments. Why can't we just get to the point? I don't have hours to waste in her office chatting."

"My colleague drives me crazy with his tangents! I don't want to brainstorm new project ideas when we haven't even finished our current project! Why can't he stay on topic in meetings? I dread meetings with him. I won't ask him to be on my next project team."

"She is so unfriendly! She never looks me in the eye when I talk to her, and she is always all business—nothing but numbers, facts, and data. Why can't she lighten up? And why can't she say good morning like a normal person?"

Unfortunately, these complaints likely do sound familiar, because at times we unconsciously undermine our relationships with our colleagues. Why? Because at work, we often focus on completing our tasks, not making friends. Which makes sense, right? We have a job to do and outcomes to deliver. However, we overlook the impact of social relationships on our ability to complete our tasks. Most of us work on teams, with vendor partners, or directly with customers. We rarely work alone.

Human beings are social animals with a fundamental need for connection. Social needs are treated the same way in the brain as the need for food and water.[1] This is why positive social interactions and relationships are considered primal needs. They also are foundational if you want to turn any job into your dream job. Work is a place where you must be social because you collaborate with others and work on teams. Social connections motivate you and fuel your innovation, creativity, and productivity.[2] And you don't want to let your emotions undermine your relationships, nor your performance. Positive relationships in the workplace are essential for our well-being and productivity.

Your next step to turn any job into your dream job is to identify where you undermine your efforts at connection and collaboration and develop new approaches and strategies so you can experience more positive social interactions and build stronger relationships.

USE THE PLATINUM RULE TO FOSTER MUTUAL RESPECT AND UNDERSTANDING

Many of us learned the Golden Rule, to treat others as you want them to treat you, as a young child. Your parents, teachers, and adults in your life knew that the Golden Rule's core virtues of empathy and compassion for others guided positive social interaction. As an adult, I learned about the *Platinum Rule* and came to realize that it more powerfully shapes positive social interaction. It suggests that you treat others the way *they* want to be treated. The Platinum Rule challenges the assumption that other people want to be treated the way you want to be treated. It also shifts your perspective from a you-centric view of social interactions to an other-centric view of social interactions. You approach people with the intention to first understand how *they* want to be treated and then adapt your interactions with them to meet their needs. The Platinum Rule is a powerful way to foster mutual respect and understanding with your professional colleagues so you can build vibrant relationships. It also can help you avoid making a negative assumption about someone's behavior, which undermines constructive social interaction.

. . .

The chief operating officer of a financial services firm hired me to help his newest managing director, Ralph, improve his leadership skills. Ralph's internal reputation was abysmal. He was described as aloof, robotic, and insensitive and as a workaholic. His team was the most disengaged team in the company, and he had the highest turnover rate. As a new leader, if Ralph did not turn around his team, he would be demoted or potentially fired.

"Ralph is cold and unfriendly, and he does not care about me as a person," Juliette, one of Ralph's team members, told me. "Each morning he walks into his office and buries his face in his two large computer monitors. My desk is directly outside of his office, and I can't remember the last time he said good morning to me as he walked into his office. It's like I'm invisible until he needs something from me. When he does need something from me, he walks into my cube and in a sentence or less asks for exactly what he needs. Then he walks out without saying another word to me. Who wants to work on a team with him? I don't."

Juliette was the seventh person I had interviewed for Ralph's 360 feedback report. As his executive coach, I needed insight from his coworkers to identify what inhibited positive relationships and constructive social interaction. Juliette's comments were consistent with what I had heard in my other interviews, and I understood how she could make negative assumptions about Ralph's behavior.

Ralph's 360 feedback confirmed for me that he followed the Golden Rule. He would treat others the way he wanted to be treated. He wanted to come to the office and get his work done. He measured his worth and success on how much work he completed in one day. He respected execution over social connection. He did not see the value in pleasantries because they were distractions and wasted time. Unfortunately, Ralph's use of the Golden Rule inhibited trust, respect, and collaboration with his team. He needed to learn and use the Platinum Rule.

I walked into Ralph's office and could see the downtown skyline through the wall of windows behind his desk. He waved at me and pointed to a chair in front of his desk and turned back to his computer to finish an email. I sat in the chair and waited. When Ralph turned to face me, there were tight lines around his eyes. I could see the muscle on the left side of his face twitch as he ground his teeth back and forth. At over six feet, four inches tall, he appeared small as he slouched down in his chair with his arms crossed over his chest.

He leaned forward and said, "I have not been looking forward to this meeting, but I know what is at stake for me and my team. I'm ready to get started."

IDENTIFY YOUR COWORKERS' WORK STYLES

To help Ralph understand how his team members and colleagues wanted to be treated, I introduced him to the concept of work styles. Your work style is the way you think about, organize, and complete your tasks.

In any office you will find four types of work styles:

- Logical, analytical, and data-oriented
- Organized, plan-focused, and detail-oriented
- Supportive, expressive, and emotionally oriented
- Strategic, integrative, and idea-oriented

Based on our work with our clients and over one million responses to the assessment I created to identify work styles,* we have discovered that the most common work styles in offices are logical, analytical, and data-oriented and organized, plan-focused, and detail-oriented. The least common work style is strategic, integrative, and idea-oriented. As you look at the descriptions of the four work styles, identify the style that best describes you and the one that best describes your boss.

> Now, you may be thinking, what if more than one of these work styles describes me and/or my boss? This is not unusual, as these four work styles are not rigidly defined or mutually exclusive. Most of us have a work style that represents a blend of these, though one work style generally tends to predominate. The goal is to use these work styles as a tool to help you interact and communicate with your colleagues based on their preferences. So if you or your boss is a blend of two work styles, you will use the recommended communication and interaction guidelines for both work styles.

---

* I designed an assessment called the Productivity Style Assessment® to help people identify their work style. If you would like to take the assessment, go to workingsimply.com/productivity-style. Or you can take the assessment in my first book, *Work Simply: Embracing the Power of Your Personal Productivity Style.*

When I asked Ralph to identify his own work style, he answered, "Logical, analytical, and data-oriented."

"And I imagine that when you work with team members, you want them to give you the facts, be direct and succinct, and get to the point in their communications with you, correct?" I asked.

Ralph nodded his head in agreement.

"What might happen if you treated and communicated with your colleagues and team members the way *they* preferred?" I asked.

Ralph flipped to the last page of his 360 feedback summary report and pointed to the feedback from Juliette and said, "Maybe my colleagues won't think I'm cold and unfriendly, and will want to work with me."

I nodded my head and told him that the first step was to identify the work style of his colleagues. In poker, players call them "tells": betting patterns or unconscious behavior you can use to guess your opponent's hand. The same rules apply to work style.

To determine the work style of a colleague, or your boss, think about the following questions:

- Does she consistently complete work early, in advance of deadlines, or wait until the last minute?

- Does he send emails with only a few words or write novels?

- Does she gesture and use her hands while talking? Or is she more controlled and stoic in her movements?

These tells, both subtle and overt, will give you clues to someone's work style.

If you need additional clues, notice the type of work that your colleagues prefer and where they excel.

- Your logical, analytical colleague is at her best when she processes data and solves complex problems. She will focus like a laser to achieve any stated goal or outcome and will ensure that you stay on budget.

- Your organized, detail-oriented colleague prefers to establish order from chaos, outline project plans, and create to-do lists. He will ensure work is completed accurately and on time.

- Your supportive, expressive colleague expertly builds relationships, facilitates team interaction, and sells ideas. She will keep all stakeholders up to date on work and effectively communicates ideas through the organization.

- Your big-picture, integrative colleague can serve as a catalyst for change, brainstorm solutions to problems, and synthesize disparate thinking. He will drive innovation, ensure variety in both thought and execution, and keep you moving forward.

Once you have identified your colleagues' work style, you want to use the Platinum Rule in your interactions with them to treat them as they want to be treated.

"Let's identify the work style of your team members. Why don't we start with Juliette who sits outside of your office? What type of work does she prefer, and where does she excel?" I asked.

"Well, she has strong relationships with everyone in the office. She knows the names of everyone's children and even what each person in the office is doing for Thanksgiving this year. She always says good morning to me and excels when she communicates and interacts with our clients. She is not in a sales role. However, she is exceptional at selling concepts and ideas. Our clients love to work with her."

"Based on these clues and cues, what is her work style?"

"Her work style is supportive, expressive, and emotionally oriented," Ralph said.

Once you have identified your team members' work style, the next step is to shift how you communicate and interact so you can treat them the way they want to be treated. The goal is to tailor your communication to the nuances of each work style so you can connect with them. The first step is to identify the preferred question that they want and need answered in every project-related interaction with you.

- Your colleague's work style that is logical, analytical, and data-oriented is focused on the *what* questions. For example, what is the goal? What do you want to achieve? What are the key facts?

- Your colleague's work style that is organized, plan-focused, and detail-oriented is focused on the *how* questions: How do you want to complete the project? How much time do you have? How has this been done in the past?

- Your colleague's work style that is supportive, expressive, and emotionally oriented is focused on the *who* questions: Who is involved? Who needs to know the information? Who will be impacted by the initiative?

- Your colleague's work style that is strategic, integrative, and idea-oriented is focused on the *why* questions: Why are we doing this project? Why this approach versus another? Why don't we consider . . . ?

TAILOR YOUR COMMUNICATION
TO YOUR COWORKERS' PREFERENCES

Once you know the primary question your colleagues want answered in their project-related interactions with you, the next step is to tailor your communication style to align with how they want to communicate.

Your logical, analytical, and data-oriented colleagues want you to focus on data and the facts. Be succinct, clear, and precise. Provide the facts without any fluff. Think through your ideas in advance and present them in a logical format. If you send an email, be direct, and technically accurate.

Your organized, plan-focused, and detail-oriented colleagues want you to stay on topic, avoid digressions, present your ideas in a sequential, organized manner, and provide detailed timelines. Provide thorough references and state any rules, procedures, or processes that may impact the project. If you send an email, outline your main points and clearly state their next action steps and the due date.

Your supportive, expressive, and emotionally oriented colleagues want the conversation to be informal, open, and warm and have no hidden agenda. They think about the impact of projects on others and how they will feel about it. They want to know who is involved in projects, and they want team members to have equal consideration when plans are being made. If you send an email, include a salutation and connect with them personally before you transition to the topic of the email.

Your strategic, integrative, and idea-oriented colleagues want you to communicate with minimal details, provide the big picture with visuals and metaphors, and articulate how the project aligns with the organization's strategy. They prefer an overview and broad conceptual framework, so limit the details. If you send an email, provide the big picture and context for the email and avoid too many details.

. . .

Once he knew how each work style preferred to communicate, Ralph understood what he could do differently to better connect and work with Juliette.

"Since Juliette's work style is supportive, expressive, and emotionally oriented, the first thing I can do differently is say good morning to her when I walk in the office," he said. "Unlike me, she won't see this as an interruption. And the next time we need to work together on a project, I'm going to discuss the overall project, ask her for her thoughts on the project's impact on our clients, and then together we will decide on what to do next."

Ralph worked hard over the next six months to change how he interacted and communicated with his team members and colleagues. He created a scorecard that listed each person's work style with detailed notes on how his coworkers wanted to be treated. At the end of each day, he reviewed his scorecard to evaluate his progress. Each Friday afternoon he sent it to me so I could celebrate his progress and support him when he got stuck. In September, 10 months after our first coaching session, the firm completed its annual employee engagement survey. The managing partner called me the day he received the results. Ralph's team had the highest score in the entire firm. And two of the firm's summer interns had requested to be on Ralph's team when they accepted their job offers.

The Golden Rule is pervasive. We unconsciously treat others the way we want to be treated. This can undermine our relationships with our colleagues and contribute to misunderstandings and negative assumptions about the behavior of others. Instead, use the Platinum Rule in your interactions with your colleagues to foster mutual respect and understanding. What is possible for you if you start to use the Platinum Rule? How much happier would you be at work? What career opportunities would be available to you? How could any job become your dream job?

DISCOVER HOW YOU UNCONSCIOUSLY UNDERMINE YOUR RELATIONSHIPS

When my new coaching client Hiroko's cell phone rang and the *Game of Thrones* theme music filled her office, I smiled. I'd found a connection with her—our mutual love of this medieval fantasy epic television show about powerful families vying for control of the Seven Kingdoms of Westeros and to sit on the Iron Throne. Over the next 15 minutes we passionately analyzed the characters and plot twists and commiserated on our disappointment in the show's finale. We transitioned easily from the politics of *Game of Thrones* to the politics and leadership challenges she experienced as a new medical director in one of the largest hospital systems in the country.

Hiroko was highly regarded professionally and personally throughout the hospital system. However, at times she would become emotionally triggered and passionately react. In the heat of the moment, her voice would rise at least two octaves, her cheeks would flush, and the more animated she became, the more her hands would move up and down and back and forth across her body.

Hiroko shared an example of a recent interactionat a meeting with her boss, Robert, and the practice manager, Maria. "I was completely blindsided. Maria told me the agenda was to discuss the new consulting model for the hospital's intensivists. It was a brief discussion, so she transitioned to a topic that was not on the agenda: how to best utilize our advanced practice providers to provide 24/7 coverage for our out of ICU patients. I was not prepared. I felt like they were making decisions about members of my team without my input. They outlined a coverage plan that I had not seen, nor been given the opportunity to provide feedback and input on. It was not fair. I told Robert that this was completely unacceptable."

"What did Robert say?"

"Well, he told me that as a physician leader, I needed to be able to dispassionately discuss topics that are emotionally triggering. He said that if I strive for future physician leadership roles, this behavior is vital. If I can't do this, then I will no longer have a seat at the leadership table. Senior leadership will realize that I cannot be objective and will make decisions without my input. Which is the last thing I want to happen!" Hiroko's voice was so loud, I'm sure the nurse in the hall heard her.

Have you ever been in a situation similar to Hiroko's where you were hijacked by your emotions? I know I have. In these moments, your heightened emotional state leads to a reaction. Maybe you raise your voice and/or get visibly angry, or maybe you completely withdraw and abandon the conversation. Almost immediately you regret what you said or did because you know that your reaction could negatively impact a relationship and/or your reputation in the office.

Our behavior is powerfully motivated by social concerns. We have a fundamental need to belong and are incredibly sensitive to our social context. And we are intensively driven to stay in our peers' good graces, so we aren't excluded from the group.[3] Which is why you feel remorse after you have an angry outburst. You have jeopardized your social position in the office. It is scary and painful.

Social pain is processed in the brain the same way as physical pain. For example, being excluded from a meeting at work "hurts" and engages very similar regions of your brain as when you are physically hurt, like when you burn your arm on the stove.[4] As a result, the motivation that drives our social behavior is designed to minimize danger and maximize reward in our brains.[5]

David Rock, cofounder of the NeuroLeadership Institute, has proposed a framework that captures the common factors that can activate your brain's risk or reward response in social situations. It's called the SCARF model and includes five domains of human experience: status, certainty, autonomy, relatedness, and fairness.[6]

Status is about your relative importance to others, or the "pecking order" or seniority in the office. It's knowing who has the most power in the room due to title. For example, have you ever attended a meeting with a client, and without anyone telling you who had the most status in the room, you knew who it was because of where she sat, how she talked, and how others in the room responded to her?

Certainty is about your need for clarity and the ability to predict the future. Our brains like to know the pattern that is occurring moment to moment. Our brains crave certainty so prediction is possible. Think about what happens to you when you don't know your manager's expectations of you or if you don't know if you might be the next person affected by your company's downsizing. Your brain becomes fixed on this uncertainty, which causes you stress and anxiety. Now think about how you feel when you hear a familiar song on the radio and sing along with the lyrics. It feels good because your brain immediately recognizes the pattern.

Autonomy is the perception that you can exert control over the events in your life and your environment. It is the sense that you have and can make choices. We have a fundamental need for control. You want and need to have choice in your life. Even if you don't feel you have any control over your work life at the moment, remember that you've made the powerful choice to step through Door Number Four so you can own, love, and make your job work for you. You are on the transformational journey to turn your job into your dream job. Autonomy is not an all-or-nothing prospect. You can start to take control just by choosing how to approach a situation, and you're already on that path.

Relatedness is your sense of connection to and security with another person. It is whether someone is perceived as similar or dissimilar to you. We naturally like to form "tribes" of people who are "like us." I grew up in South Carolina with two strong Atlantic Coast Conference (ACC) football teams, the University of South Carolina and Clemson University. Columbia, my hometown, was sharply divided between diehard Gamecocks fans (University of South Carolina) and Tigers fans (Clemson University). Watch out if you showed up to a party on a Saturday in the fall and cheered for the wrong team. You were quickly excluded from the social group.

Lastly, *fairness* refers to a just and nonbiased exchange between people. It's about a perception of a fair exchange between people. In the meeting with Maria and Robert, Hiroko did not think it was a fair exchange. Maria and Robert were both prepared for the discussion, and she was not. In our coaching session, Hiroko told me that she believed her lack of preparation for the discussion put her at an unfair disadvantage where she could not effectively advocate for her advanced practice providers. In this social situation Hiroko's danger response was triggered, and she reacted emotionally.

In my coaching and consulting work, my team and I use the SCARF model extensively. We do this because you don't want your emotions to hijack you and negatively impact your relationships and interactions with your professional colleagues. To have more positive social interactions and build supportive relationships, you first need to identify what activates your brain's danger response in social situations.

IDENTIFY AND MITIGATE SCARF THREATS

Each of us has a primary SCARF threat that when triggered causes us either to respond with an angry, aggressive outburst or to become silent and withdraw from the situation. My primary SCARF threat is autonomy. The perception or reality that I don't have control or choice over the events in my life causes me to shut down and withdraw from the person or conversation, and at times leads to an outburst of anger. My first job after college was at a bank. The hours were long, and I could not leave the office until my manager, Jim, left for the day. This was before the launch of social media. It was before the Internet had billions of fascinating things to look at—when the only things you found when you surfed the Interned were weird white papers and forums that were not that interesting. Bored, with no control over my schedule, I would sit in my beige cubicle and hope, pray, and wish Jim would leave so I could go out with my friends or just go to bed.

One afternoon, I asked Jim if I could leave early. I had a hair appointment at 8:00 p.m. Maybe it is because I was born and raised in the South, but hair appointments are sacred events that you do not miss, or cancel. Close to 7:00 p.m., Jim gave me another PowerPoint deck to revise. By 7:20 p.m. I was frantic. If I did not leave the office by 7:25 p.m., I would not be on time for my hair appointment. At 7:22 p.m. I walked over to Jim's desk with 5 of the revised slides and told him I would be in early the next morning to finish the other 20 slides. He looked at me and said I could not leave until the slides were finished. In that moment I completely lost it.

I looked at him, and in what my family and friends now call my outside voice, I shouted, "Have you seen my hair? I cannot miss my hair appointment tonight! I'm leaving!"

Jim's eyes got wide; then he blinked twice and said, "You are leaving for a hair appointment?"

"Yes! The slides will be on your desk in the morning," I screamed as I sprinted for the elevator.

I arrived at the office at 4:15 a.m. the next morning, and the updated slides were on Jim's desk when he arrived. However, I had lost credibility with Jim. He included the outburst in my annual performance review with a note about my lack of professionalism and respect. It was months before I regained Jim's trust and repaired our relationship. My SCARF threat hijacked the rational part of my brain and led to unproductive, unprofessional behavior. When I left the bank a few years later, Jim wished me good luck in my new job and with a big grin on his face reminded me to avoid another "hair gate" instance with my new boss.

What is your primary SCARF threat? Is it status, certainty, autonomy, relatedness, or fairness? As you read the descriptions above, did any of them make you say "Yes, absolutely"? Or "That is exactly what I feel"? Or "That is what I always think about in my interactions with others"?

The first way to determine your primary SCARF threat is to listen to your instincts or gut reaction to each description. Your instincts are correct. Listen to what they tell you. If you still are unsure, reflect on prior conversations or situations where you got angry or withdrew and look for your trigger clues. Was it a word or phrase that someone said that made you feel less than or that the person was talking down to you? That is status hazard. Maybe you notice a pattern where you are anxious if you don't know what to expect or what will be discussed. That is a certainty menace. Or you may notice that you are consistently triggered because you don't have the flexibility in your schedule to attend your child's school events. That is an autonomy risk. Or you notice that when you are not included in meetings or asked out to lunch by your colleagues you withdraw. That is a relatedness danger. Or you may be triggered when someone monopolizes the conversation and does not allow other people to speak or you are paid less than your colleague whose job is the same as your job. That is a fairness hazard.

Now that you know your primary SCARF threat, the second step for more positive social interactions and supportive relationships is to minimize SCARF threats, both yours and, when possible, your colleagues'.

It is easy to trigger a status violation. Think about the last time someone gave you instructions, corrected you on a task, or asked if they could give you feedback. You probably felt less than the other person. To counter a status risk in yourself, reframe the situation and think about the feedback or instructions as a way to improve your individual performance. Shift your perspective from you versus them, which triggers a status peril, to you versus you. The instruction is intended to help you grow, develop, and/or learn a new skill.

If you need to provide feedback to a colleague, first ask for their feedback on their own performance and then share your thoughts. For example, my chief of staff, Wendelyn, had developed email templates to make it easier for us to respond to frequently asked questions. There were a few edits I wanted to suggest that she make. I scheduled a meeting with her to review the email templates and asked her for her feedback on each template first. After she shared her thoughts on how to improve the templates, I used the phrase "yes, and" and shared my ideas to improve the templates. When I said "Yes, and," I acknowledged her feedback, shared mine as additive to her feedback, and avoided a status hazard. Now, you and your colleague are equals on an even playing field.

Your brain craves certainty. It wants to know the pattern occurring moment to moment so it can predict what is next. Anything that is unexpected or does not follow a pattern can trigger a certainty vulnerability. Hiroko experienced a certainty danger in her meeting with Maria and Robert. The agenda was to discuss the new consulting model for the intensivists. When it shifted to how to provide 24/7 coverage for the out of ICU patients, it did not follow the pattern outlined in the original agenda.

To reduce or eliminate a certainty risk, ask for a meeting agenda, clarify the topic of the meeting or discussion with your boss, in advance. If you are working on a team, break the project down into small, discrete action steps with due dates. Discuss and agree to project working agreements, explicitly outline how you will manage project meetings, and establish what you will do if the project derails. Decide in advance how you will address the roadblocks and problems that are inherent in any project. You and your brain will relax once you know what to expect.

At work, autonomy hazards can be pervasive. Micromanagement, as I experienced with my boss George (remember, you met him in Chapter One; he was the one who called my husband to see if I was at home sick), is too common in many of our workplaces. When you sense a lack of control or the inability to influence an outcome, your brain screams out danger. Proactively identify where you do have autonomy at work. It could be as simple as how you arrange your workspace, your ability to choose which projects you work on when and with whom, or your ability to direct your own learning through your organization's learning management system. To minimize autonomy perils when you work on a team, present options and ask for input from the team. Look for places where you can offer choice and control to your colleagues. The perception of choice calms the brain.

We naturally like to form teams or silos with people who are like us at work to create a sense of belonging or relatedness. In our global economy you may work on a team with colleagues from a different culture, and you may never meet in person. However, if someone is not on the team or is different from you, your brain can decide that they not are related and create a hazard response.

To mitigate the automatic "foe" response, look for places of similarity with your colleagues. Share personal stories, experiences, or photos that build social connection with your team members. When one of my executive coaching clients was promoted, she became the leader of a virtual, global team. To build connections and camaraderie among her team members, she began each team meeting with a personal icebreaker. For example, team members shared their favorite holiday tradition, their perfect birthday meal, and their favorite TV show. If you work on a large team, divide the team into smaller groups. Smaller groups appear safer than larger groups. And if you have colleagues spread across the globe, use videoconferencing technology for your meetings so team members can see their colleagues and read nonverbal cues. A smile is a universal, nonthreatening language that allows your brain to relax.

A danger response from unfairness can easily be activated. Hiroko was triggered within the first 10 minutes of her meeting with Maria and Robert. Maria and Robert could have mitigated or eliminated this trigger if they had included on the agenda that they would also discuss the advanced practice providers coverage plan. Transparency is one of the most powerful tools you can use to alleviate the unfairness trigger in your colleagues. Just like clear expectations, working agreements, procedures, and processes enhance certainty, they also boost fairness. When you work on a team, discuss how you will decide who completes which tasks and how you will manage the collective and individual workload. This will ensure that a fair exchange of work occurs for all members of the team.

STOP MAKING NEGATIVE ASSUMPTIONS ABOUT YOUR COLLEAGUES' BEHAVIOR AND GET OFF THE LADDER OF INFERENCE

The Ladder of Inference[7] is a theory developed by Chris Argyris. There are six rungs on the Ladder of Inference, and like a ladder, the higher up you go, the farther away you are from the facts of what really happened in the interaction. As you climb the ladder, you make inferences about the other person's behavior and intentions. Then you develop an opinion or story about the person's behavior. You seek and embrace information that confirms your opinion or story and ignore or reject information that casts doubt on or negates your opinion. This is called confirmation bias. When you are under the influence of confirmation bias, you do not perceive circumstances objectively. You select the parts of conversations, interactions, or pieces of data that make you feel good because they confirm your opinions. This creates discord, conflict, and mistrust in relationships.

. . .

"I know that Maria and Robert intentionally blindsided me in the meeting," Hiroko explained. "They don't value me or respect me as a physician leader. This is not the first time that I have attended a meeting where they have brought up a topic that was not on the original agenda *and* that they have previously discussed. Maria and Robert make decisions without my input all the time. Two weeks ago, they changed our attending holiday call schedule without any feedback from me. I have talked to Robert about all of this before, and nothing changes. I'm going to talk to the president of our division and let him know what I think about the proposed advanced practice provider coverage plan."

I nodded my head as I listened to Hiroko. She was in very familiar territory. She had made inferences about Maria and Robert's behavior. She had decided to act based on the story she created in her mind about their intentions. Hiroko had climbed the Ladder of Inference.

The journey up the Ladder of Inference begins with an interaction with another person or multiple people. It can be a brief exchange in the hallway, an email, a one-on-one conversation, or a meeting with a group of people. Then you progress up the six rungs:

The first rung: You filter out some information, dialogue, or facts. When you filter out some of these things, you overlook the facts of what actually happened in the interaction. This sets up the conditions to make an inference about the person or the people involved in the interaction. For example, Hiroko filtered out how difficult it is to coordinate two physicians and a practice manager's calendar to schedule a meeting. The meeting was scheduled for 45 minutes, and the agenda items were covered in 20 minutes. Maria and Robert decided to use the remaining time to address additional topics while they had all the decision makers in the room and avoid a second meeting.

The second rung: You experience fear. Your brain's fear response is triggered, and you experience a SCARF—a threat to status, certainty, autonomy, relatedness, and/or fairness. For example, Hiroko experienced a certainty and status violation. Her certainty was jeopardized because she was unprepared and did not expect to discuss advanced practice provider coverage at this meeting. She also experienced a status risk. She felt her position as a medical director was discounted because Maria and Robert had discussed advanced practice provider coverage prior to this meeting without her.

The third rung: You make a negative inference about the other person's intentions. You assume that the person's actions were not honorable. You may tell yourself that she is disrespectful, or that he does not care whether this upsets you, or that she does not care how it impacts those on your team or your direct reports. For example, Hiroko made multiple negative inferences about Maria and Robert's behavior. She inferred that they had intentionally blindsided her and they did not value her or respect her position as a medical director.

The fourth rung: You become entrenched in your position. You are certain you're right. You tell yourself that the other people do not get it and that they should change. You are right, and "they" are wrong. You may tell yourself that we've talked about this so many times, but nothing changes. So obviously the other people do not have good intentions. For example, Hiroko believed that she was right, that Maria and Robert did not understand, and that it was up to Maria and Robert to change.

The fifth rung: You connect past behavior. You couple this experience with other things you believe to be true. You look at the others' past behavior and connect it to the current situation. You may tell yourself that you keep trying to get "them" to see their behavior and the impact of it on other people. But "they" keep doing the same thing. Obviously, "they" can't be influenced. For example, Hiroko said that this was not the first time that she had been blindsided by Maria and Robert. They had made decisions without her. She immediately recalled a situation where the attending holiday call schedule was changed without her input.

The sixth rung: You act based on the story in your head. At this point you may avoid the other people, you may work around them, you may argue with them, or you may talk to others about how impossible they are to work with or work for. For example, Hiroko decided to work around both Maria and Robert and go to the president of the division to discuss her concerns about the proposed advanced practice provider coverage. This decision is politically risky for Hiroko. It could erode trust in her relationship with Robert, negatively impact her brand if she is perceived as a non-team player, and potentially limit future leadership opportunities for her. It was imperative that Hiroko get off the ladder and not make decisions, nor act based on the inferences she had made about Maria, Robert, and the situation.

• • •

Now that you can see the dangers of climbing the Ladder of Inference, it's time to improve your communication and relationships with others and get off the Ladder of Inference through reflection, support, and inquiry.

We discussed the power of *reflection* and how journaling can be used as a reflection tool in Chapter Four. *(Go to pages 72–74 to revisit the directions on how to journal.) Support* is when you share your thinking and reasoning with a friend, a coach, a mentor, or a trusted colleague to gain a different perspective and to test your conclusions and assumptions. And *inquiry* is when you engage in a conversation to inquire into the other person's thinking and reasoning.

To get Hiroko off the Ladder of Inference, first we reflected on the meeting together and tested her conclusions. Then I suggested that she have a conversation with Robert to understand his perspective on the meeting, and to explore her assumptions about his behavior and beliefs about her as a leader. To help Hiroko prepare for her conversation with Robert, we walked through her conversation with Robert using the five steps below:

1. **Cite what you heard or saw.** Give a neutral, respectful account that does not include opinions or inferences. Start the conversation with any of the following statements: "I think . . . ," "I think I heard you say . . . ," or "I think I saw . . ." When you begin with "I think," you leave room for the possibility that you may have filtered out or overlooked some information or data. And when you use "I" versus "you" to open the conversation, you do not put the other person on the defensive so the person can be receptive to you.

    Hiroko thought for a moment and then said, "I think that the topic of advanced practice provider coverage was not on the original agenda that was included in the meeting request for last Tuesday's meeting." This is a neutral statement, it implies that she may have overlooked a topic on the agenda, and it can be fact-checked against the meeting agenda included in the meeting request.

2. **Assume and grant honorable intentions.** Be open to the possibility that there was a decent reason why the behavior or situation occurred.

    Hiroko pondered for a moment and then thought about prior meetings with Maria and Robert. She discovered multiple meetings where they followed the agenda and did not introduce topics that were not on the agenda. When she identified instances where they had not "blindsided" her, it was easier to assume and grant an honorable intention for their behavior in this specific meeting.

3. **Ask for what you missed.** Remember, everyone filters stuff out. Your objective is to learn new information that will provide the context or reason behind the behavior or interaction. Think of yourself as an explorer on a search for new information.

    After Hiroko stated that she thought the topic of advanced practice provider coverage was not on the agenda, she asked, "What did I miss?"

4. **Compare perceptions and stories so you can check your confirmation bias.** Listen to the response you receive to your "What did I miss?" question. You want to focus on facts versus your perceptions and stories. Facts are actual occurrences that can be proved through observation or measurement. Stories are judgments, conclusions, or

attributions that you make from the facts. Judgments evaluate whether the fact is good or bad. Conclusions are how you connect and interpret the facts. And attributions are how you determine why people do what they do.

To check your confirmation bias, begin the next part of the conversation with the phrase "The story I told myself" and insert your perception of the situation. When you use the phrase, "the story I told myself" you acknowledge that it may not be true and signify that you are open to the possibility that your perception is not an accurate reflection of the other person's intention.

Hiroko then stated, "The story I told myself was that you intentionally blindsided me because you did not value and respect me as a leader."

Continue to check your perspective and their perspective with the phrase "I'm thinking . . . . How does that compare with what you're thinking?"

Hiroko continued, "I'm thinking that you and Maria saw an opportunity to discuss an important topic, patient care and coverage, and took it. How does that compare with what you're thinking?"

5. **Listen. Then suggest an action focused on shared mutual interests.** At this point in the conversation, you will ask for what you need and suggest a path forward that aligns and supports what you both want. Use the phrase, "I think it would be helpful to us if (*action*), because (*mutual interest*). How does that match up with what you want?"

Hiroko continued, "I think it would be helpful to us in the future if there is a topic that is not on the original agenda that is brought up that we pause the meeting and allow everyone time to think about the topic, because then each person would be able to provide thoughtful feedback in the meeting. How does that match up with what you want?"

. . .

When Hiroko and I finished walking through the five steps to get off the Ladder of Inference, I asked her if she was prepared for her conversation with Robert on Thursday afternoon. She nodded her head and smiled.

Three weeks later I received an email from Robert that said, "After Hiroko and I met, I understood why she felt blindsided in the meeting with me and Maria. I told her that though it is optimal that one knows the agenda prior to a meeting, it is not always possible. And spontaneous discussion can have value. I reiterated that I needed her as a physician leader to be able to dispassionately discuss topics that produce internal strife and strong emotions. Yesterday, Hiroko, myself, the president of our division, and the president of the children's hospital met to discuss significant changes to Hiroko's program, staffing, and reporting structure. It was an emotionally charged meeting. The political stakes were high. Hiroko was calm, and unlike at previous meetings, she did not 'draw lines in the sand.' She was able to expand her perspective and think globally about the changes and the implications for the entire healthcare system. And she compromised on an important issue. I praised and acknowledged her after the meeting for this new and valuable behavior. The good news is I see the improvement in her behavior. And know she has future leadership potential." When Hiroko's one-year term as medical director ended, Robert recommended her for a second term, which she accepted.

Small, incremental shifts are life changing. Identify the work style of your colleagues and boss, use the Platinum Rule in your interactions with them, or recognize your SCARF threats or notice when you climb up the Ladder of Inference. Own and embrace your power to mitigate SCARF threats and climb back down the Ladder of Inference. You have everything you need to make a slight adjustment to profoundly change your relationships. Enjoy the vibrant relationships you create that can turn any job into your dream job.

STEP THREE

—MAKE IT WORK.—
MAKE YOUR JOB WORK FOR YOU

DESIGN your work to find *your* meaning

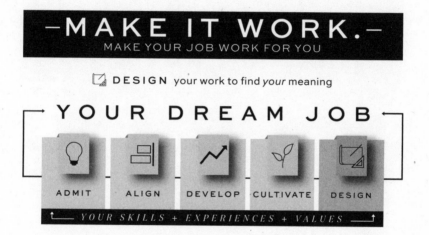

YOUR DREAM JOB

ADMIT · ALIGN · DEVELOP · CULTIVATE · DESIGN

YOUR SKILLS + EXPERIENCES + VALUES

Think back to when you made the powerful decision to walk through Door Number Four in Chapter Two. You selected the path of possibility and choice so you could turn any job into your dream job. Now, look at how far you have come! You faced your fear and used it to focus on what really mattered to you. You owned your power in the relationship with your employer and admitted your recognition and appreciation needs. To shape your life to meet your professional and personal aspirations, you aligned your strengths to your company's goals. You rekindled passion and joy in your work so you could really love what you do. To advance in your career you developed new skills and knowledge. And you made your professional relationships stronger, more nurturing, and more authentic.

That is incredible! Make sure you take the time to stop, pause, and celebrate your hard work. Look at all that you have accomplished. Way to go!

Your final lap on your transformational journey is here. Now you are ready to go deeper and find your meaning in your work.

CHAPTER SEVEN

DESIGN YOUR JOB TO FIND *YOUR* MEANING

Remember how I called my college cross-country coach, Coach Phemister, to help me deal with my boss, George, who called my husband to find out if I left work early because I was sick? As you may recall, this conversation inspired me to reframe my job selling booth space for a home and garden show as a place to develop and refine my sales skills. This worked for a while, and I was even promoted. However, the work continued to feel transactional and sterile. Something was still missing. Where was the value and meaning in my work? Was it even possible for a sales job to have a purpose beyond making money? And did it really matter if my job had meaning? What, if anything, would change for me if my job had significance beyond a paycheck?

On my way to work one cold, dark February morning, I heard an economics professor on National Public Radio say that all work had meaning. He said that all businesses create and provide products and services that provide real benefits; otherwise people would not buy them. I remember thinking that was a logical argument. The exposition company I worked for that produced home and garden shows could not have been in business for over 40 years if no one bought what it sold.

For the rest of the drive, I thought about Tammy, who sold "squirrel-proof" bird feeders. On the large TV in the center of her booth space she showed videos of squirrels trying, unsuccessfully, to fit their paws into the small crevices of her bird feeder. And I thought about Cheryl's booth walls adorned with gorgeous pictures of backyard ponds filled with goldfish and water lilies and small waterfalls cascading over gray craggy rocks that she had installed in her customers' yards. I thought about the benefits of the booth space I sold. However, as soon as I pulled into the company parking lot, thoughts of my mile-long to-do list jolted me from my existential reflection. It was back to the unfulfilling grind.

A few weeks later, as I reviewed my sales to date and my warm prospect list, I realized that more than 90 percent of my customers and prospects were small business owners in their first or second year of business who operated without a storefront. And most of them were women. I recognized, for the first time, the value I provided.

An inexpensive physical space with consistent, high-volume traffic enabled these new entrepreneurs to market, sell, and test their products and services. In that moment, I reframed and redefined how I thought about and experienced my work. I shifted from thinking about my work as a transactional telemarketer of 10×10 booth space to an enabler of small business growth and innovation. I helped and supported women, women like my Mom who also was a small business owner, achieve their business dreams. This was a purpose beyond my paycheck. I had defined the meaning in my work.

. . .

The value and importance of your work is defined by *you*. Meaning is not controlled by what happens in your life. It is made by your interpretation of the events in your life. Your inner self-talk shapes, constructs, and defines it. Since we all view the world through a different lens, it is impossible to provide a universal, one-size-fits-all definition of meaningful work. It is too subjective. Meaning is what you bring to the table. It is uniquely yours. No one can define it for you.

You can find meaning in *any* job because *you* define it. No jobs are exempt from significance. To identify the value in your work, think about the context of work in your life. For example, work is a paycheck, or it's a higher calling, or it's a form of creative expression. You can find worth in your work through your interactions with other people by being on a team united around a common purpose or expressing common values and beliefs. Substance can be found in the context or nature of the work, the tasks you perform, the organization's mission or commitment to the environment, sustainability, or community service.

When you change how you frame your work's purpose, you change the meaning of your work and transform how you define yourself as a doer of the work.[1] Once I no longer saw myself as a transactional telemarketer, my work experience radically changed. To be an enabler of small business growth inspired, energized, and motivated me. My job was no longer a grind. When my alarm went off on Monday mornings, I did not hit snooze five times. I wanted to get out of bed and go to work. I *needed* to be at my desk because my work mattered to the small business owners I served.

You spend more than one-third of your waking life at work. Whether work has the starring role, is a small player, or is the hero or villain in your life completely depends on *you* and your relationship to your work. Now is the time for you to step powerfully and confidently into the deeper why of your work. The final step in your journey to own, love, and make your job work for you is to design your job to find *your* meaning.

IS YOUR WORK A JOB, A CAREER, OR A CALLING?

Almost once a week, for the past 10 years, I have taught a corporate training class. During this time, I've observed that there are three types of people who attend my workshops: prisoners, participants, and students.

The prisoners make it known that they are only in the workshop because it is a mandatory requirement. Prisoners do what is minimally required to receive "credit" for the class, while they check their smartphones and count down the minutes to the next break or the end of the day.

The participants are in the workshop because they need the knowledge, skills, or experience to advance their career. They often sit near their manager or a person with higher status or power to develop or strengthen a connection with them. Participants thoughtfully answer my questions and are careful to ensure that their workshop engagement elevates their brand and reputation.

The students are in the workshop because they want to grow. They want to learn a new skill and/or explore an alternative perspective, approach, or idea that may help them in their career.

A few months ago, after coaching three people who were the same age and gender and also held the same position and occupation, I recognized that people who do the same work can and do experience that work differently. Just as there are three different types of people and experiences in my training classes, people relate to their work in three distinct ways. Isn't it liberating to realize that you have control over your experiences?

You have the power and can design your job to derive more significance from it. In order to make that happen for you, let's start with an awareness of where you are right now. Why? Because all change starts with an awareness of your current connection to your work.

Read the paragraphs below and decide if any of them describe your current affiliation to work. You might read one paragraph and find that it explains exactly how you connect to your work. Or you might read them all and realize that you relate to your work as a combination of two or three. That is fine. Stay focused on the goal and identify how *you* relate to your work today.

If you connect to your work as a job, it is a necessity of life. It is how you pay the bills. Your job is how you support your life, hobbies, and interests outside of work.[2] You do not seek or receive any other reward from it. You live for 5 p.m., the weekend, and your next vacation. And if you were asked if you would enter this profession again, or encourage your family or friends to enter this profession, you say no, probably "Hell no!"

If you relate to your work as a career, the focus is on achievement and advancement. For example, if you meet a person who relates to their work as a career at a networking event and ask them what they do, they might tell you what they do in the context of their accomplishments. "I lead Talent for my company and report to the board of directors on our progress. I also lead HR for our corporate office, and report to our general counsel (chief legal officer) but take most of my direction directly from our CEO. I am the most senior person in HR now, and really enjoy my role." If your work is a career, you probably don't expect to be in your current job in a few years because you plan to move on to a better, higher-level job. A promotion is a recognition that you have outperformed your coworkers.[3]

If you relate to your work as a calling, work is not for financial gain or career advancement. Work is a source of fulfillment. It is one of the most important parts of your life and a vital part of who you are. At parties your work is one of the first things you tell people about yourself. If you won the lottery today, you would still do your work. You probably dread the thought of retirement and have encouraged friends and family members to join this profession. You love your work and believe it makes the world a better place.[4]

It is probably not a surprise to you that people who relate to their work as a calling experience greater life, better health, and job satisfaction.[5] You might be thinking that only people in "passion" professions can and do experience work as a calling. You must be an artist, writer, teacher, nurse, minister, etc., to relate to your work as a calling. I hear you. However, I have seen with our clients, in my own company, and with my colleagues and friends that this simply isn't true. You can relate to your job as a calling *regardless* of occupation, age, income, and education.

You define how you experience your work. If you want your job to be more than a transactional necessity, it can be. If you want your career to have purpose beyond your next promotion, it can. If you want your calling to have deeper, richer meaning, it can. However, in order to make that happen, you have to acknowledge that you have the power to create a professional life that aligns with who you are and how you choose to make an impact in and for the world.

DESIGN YOUR WORK FOR MORE MEANING

Celia is the unit secretary in the Pediatric Intensive Care Unit in one of the largest hospital systems in the country. She answers the phone, coordinates physician and therapeutic consultations, and ensures that deliveries go to the correct nurse, patient, or family member. The work she performs is transactional and administrative. However, that is *not* how Celia experiences her work.

"I am the Mother Hen of this floor. All the people I work with are my children. I care for them so they can care for our patients. I am the concierge for our patients' families. If they need anything, I will get it for them. I also help care for our patients. I make sure that medications get to the nurses from our pharmacy system," Celia told me when I interviewed her for this book.

Celia views her job as a valuable whole that positively impacts other people, not a collection of separate tasks. She proactively and intentionally designed her work to derive meaning from it. How?

She modified and extended the scope and nature of a unit secretary's responsibilities to support a broader purpose in her work. She even took on additional duties that align with how she experiences and relates to her work as the "Mother Hen" of the floor.

"I asked the medical director if I could be responsible for stocking the refrigerator and snacks in the breakroom. Food services doesn't know what my nurses, physicians, and team members like and need. I do. I take care of them so they can take care of our patients. Twice a month, I do an inventory and ask the members of the team what they need or if they want anything special. I shop on my way home from work and bring the drinks and food in the next morning," Celia said.

To do significant work requires that you take action to make your job requirements feed a broader purpose. You must be an active designer and creator of your professional experience. You can shape your vocation to fit your own unique orientation and bond with it. You have the power to structure your job differently to create value in your work.

It's time for you to take the reins, and in order to do so, you must make behavioral, relational, and/or psychological changes to how you work and/or to how you relate to your work.

There are three areas where you can shape your work: task, relational, and cognitive,[6] and each one involves specific types of modifications you can make to how you work.

- **Task.** You make behavioral changes to *how* you perform your set of assigned job activities. Either you adjust the scope or nature of assignments involved in your job, or you take on additional responsibilities.

- **Relational.** You make changes to your professional relationships. Either you alter the extent or nature of your affiliation with the people you currently work with, or you develop and build new associations.

- **Cognitive.** You make proactive psychological changes to your perceptions of your job. You redefine what you see as the type or nature of the duties or relationships involved in your job. And you reframe your job to see it as a meaningful whole that positively impacts others rather than a collection of separate responsibilities.[7]

So, what does it look like to make task, relational, and cognitive changes at work? Let's dive deeper into each area to find out.

Task Changes

You have two options to adjust the tasks in your job.

The first option is to modify either their scope or their nature. For example, Ava is the project manager at a national construction supply company, and one of her responsibilities is to ensure that the construction team uses high-quality products on its projects. While researching innovative building supply materials, she would explore and brainstorm marketing opportunities for the company, which was not part of her job. However, because she was interested in it, she used this as an opportunity to modify the scope and nature of her job.

The second option to alter your tasks at work is to take on one or more additional responsibilities. For example, in her meetings with the sales team, the owner of the company, or the project site supervisors, Ava now shares a promotional idea for how to use the product selections to differentiate the company from its competition.

In Chapter Four you excavated your strengths and used them to shape your work to meet your personal and professional goals. Now go one step further and use your strengths to make your work have more value. Refer to your list of strengths from Chapter Four and answer the questions below for each strength:

1. What job duty could I modify so that I can more fully use my strengths to add more meaning to my job?

2. What strength am I not using that I want to use to unlock more significance in my work? What task could I add to use this strength and find more value in my work?

Review your answers to each question and find the job responsibility that you can modify without the approval of your manager. Then, just do it! How good does that feel? For other assignments that need input from your manager, schedule a meeting to discuss what you want to do and how it will benefit both you and the company.

Relational Changes

Now let's explore how you can alter your professional relationships.

Your first option is to change the extent or nature of an existing relationship. For example, Joe, an associate at an insurance company, adjusted his relationship with his manager, Susan. "I've limited some of my interactions with Susan because she will spend hours in meetings going over and over quote details. For example, we've had meetings that last two or three hours on a quote that we could have discussed in just one hour. So now, if there is a meeting scheduled to review a quote, I know I should schedule another meeting to start one hour after my meeting with Susan. This ensures that our meeting ends on time and that the quote review is complete. This has saved me hours, and I don't think Susan has really noticed because all my quotes have been completed correctly and submitted on time."

You can also develop new connections to derive more meaning from your work. For example, Jill is the second highest ranking woman in a global manufacturing firm. She has achieved extraordinary success and is three years away from retirement. At our last executive coaching session, she said to me, "We have been discussing my career, my legacy, and the imprint I want to leave on this company. I decided I want to support, develop, and advocate for women. Of course, it is outside of my day-to-day responsibilities; however, this is important, significant work to me. Once I made this decision, I met with Nicole, who leads our Women's Connect group, and now I am helping her plan the group's upcoming networking event in March. I also worked with my HR generalist and identified the top 15 high-potential women in my business. Now, when I am in a city where one of them works, I take them out to lunch or to dinner to get to know them better and learn how I can help them advance in their careers. I've never felt more engaged and alive!"

Now, it's your turn to brainstorm how you might modify a professional relationship.

1. Identify the five to seven people with whom you interact the most frequently in your job. You want to focus on these people, because if you change one of these relationships, it can make a significant, positive impact on your experience at work. This could be your manager, your coworker who sits next to you, or a person from a different department who is on a project team with you.

2. At the top of a sheet of paper, write the name of one of the people you've just identified. Draw two lines horizontally to divide the paper into thirds. Then draw a line to divide the paper vertically, stopping at the second horizonal line on the paper. Do not draw a line through the second horizontal line. You now have four square quadrants and a rectangle below them. In the upper-left quadrant, draw a plus sign (+). In the upper-right quadrant, draw a plus sign and an up arrow. In the lower-left quadrant, draw a minus sign (−). In the lower-right quadrant, draw a minus sign and a down arrow. You can see an example of what your page should look like in the figure.

Sally Wells, Manager

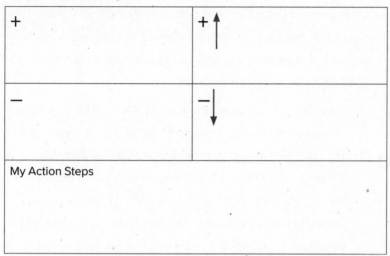

3. The upper-left quadrant represents the positive aspects of your relationship with this person. In this box list all the positive benefits and value you encounter when you interact with this person.

4. The upper-right quadrant represents the positive aspects of your relationship that you want to experience more often. In this box list what you want more of in this relationship.

5. The lower-left quadrant represents the negative aspects of the affiliation with this person. In this box list the negative interactions that have undermined your fulfillment and joy at work. You might not have any undesirable experiences with this person. If so, skip this box.

6. The lower-right quadrant represents the unconstructive aspects of the relationship you want to have less often. In this box list what you want less of in your interactions with this person. This can be something you want to stop completely, or just minimize.

7. Now, in the horizontal box at the bottom of the page, write down two action steps you will take to change your rapport with this person. I suggest that one action step enable what you want more of in this relationship and the other action step support what you want less of. For example, remember how Joe limited his interactions with Susan? He intentionally scheduled a meeting to start one hour after the start time of his meetings with Susan. This was a small, simple modification. Don't underestimate the power of incremental adjustments. Small changes quickly add up. They can fundamentally shift relationships without radical, jarring change, which makes them feel and be less risky. An example of the completed exercise is below.

8. Complete the steps above for each person you identified to modify your current relationship.

Sally Wells, Manager

+	+ ↑
• Interpersonal skills. Warm, vibrant, and personable. It is helpful to bring her to client meetings because clients enjoy interacting with her. • Strategic, big-picture thinker. Helps me "think outside the box." • Understands who the internal, external, stated, and implied stakeholders are for each team project. It is easier to navigate the company politics with this information. • Advocates for me and my career. Helps me identify opportunities to develop as a leader in the organization.	• Advocates for me and my career. Helps me identify opportunities to develop as a leader in the organization.
—	**— ↓**
• Dumps and runs. Delegates too many projects at one time and does not provide deadlines. I work nights and weekends to get the work done. • Late. Does not arrive on time for meetings. I am always late for any meeting I have after I meet with her. • Lack of process orientation. Does not understand the sequencing of tasks within a project. I have to rework project plans and correct mistakes because tasks were not completed in order.	• Dumps and runs. Delegates too many projects at one time and does not provide deadlines. I work nights and weekends to get the work done.

Action Steps I Will Take

Discuss the company's leadership development program with Sally and ask if she will nominate me to participate in it.

When Sally delegates a task for a deadline, I will ask her to help me prioritize the other tasks she has previously assigned to me.

You now have a road map to modify a professional relationship.

The second option to alter your professional relationships is to develop new professional connections. Your first step is to identify a passion you want to pursue, a special interest you have, an experience you want to have, or a new skill you want to develop that will help you derive more significance from your work. Then find the person or people who can help you. You may have to do some research on the company's intranet site, talk to a coworker, or search LinkedIn to identify the right person. Once you know who can help you, reach out to that person and ask for the person's support.

Now, it might seem awkward, politically risky, or just extremely uncomfortable to reach out to people you don't know or who are in a more senior position than you. I get it. However, when our clients reach out to people they don't know in their company, they consistently receive enthusiastic support and encouragement. Still on the fence? Think about it this way. If you reach out to people because of a passion and interest to join, support, or advocate on behalf of a project or a cause, why would they turn you away? They need and want your participation. Your interest in their project or cause also validates its importance. When you reach out to others to learn more about their work, skills, or career, you reinforce their worth and contributions to the company.

Cognitive Changes

The final place you can design your work is cognitively, which is how you define and relate to your work. When you do this, you reframe your job to see it as an important whole that positively impacts others rather than a collection of separate to-dos.

How? Expand the lens through which you observe your work. You want to zoom out so you can look at your responsibilities as a collection of tasks, not a set of individual duties. Don't focus on just one aspect of your work, and don't look at a single to-do task in isolation. Each task is part of a greater whole. It is the composite of them all that has the value and purpose for you.

To see the collective whole of your work, list all your job accountabilities. For each one, ask yourself the question, "So what?" This question acts as a way for you to identify the importance or significance of each duty. For example, when I sold booth space at home and garden shows, my job description stated "Make a minimum of 50 outbound sales calls a week." So what? My answer to that was "To market our trade show to as many business owners as possible and to introduce business owners to trade shows as an option to sell their products and services." That's a lot more inspiring than "Make 50 outbound sales calls."

After you have answered the "So what?" question for each of your tasks, look at your answers. Is there a theme or a common link among them all? Is there a primary objective or goal of your work? In my work, the objective or goal was to produce a trade show where business owners could sell their products and services to a targeted group of people who had an interest in and/or need for them. How would you describe the central objective of your work?

With this information in mind, you are now ready to uncover the meaning in your work and identify how your work positively impacts other people. Below are a few questions to consider. You might want to write down your answers or think about them and then discuss them with a friend, a coworker, or your spouse or partner.

- Why do people buy your product or service?
- What is the benefit your customers receive from using your product or service?
- What would happen if your product or service did not exist? For your customer? For your community?
- How do you positively affect people?

Your final step is to write a meaning statement for your work. For example, the meaning statement in my sales job was "I help small business owners achieve their business dreams." I encourage you to write your meaning statement down and post it where you can see it. Why? Because we all have bad days. There will still be something you don't like. Your manager may "check in" on you for the third time in an hour, or the scent of your cubemate's lunch may still permeate the cubicle you share the next day. Or you may still have to complete the long, detailed report no one reads. It is in these moments that a visual reminder of why you and your work matter is important.

When I was still working for George selling booth space for home and garden shows, I found myself in a two-month stretch where people hung up on me almost every other cold sales call, I actively disliked what was on my to-do list, and George was being even more of a micromanager jerk. I had reached my limit, so I wrote my meaning statement on a Post-it Note and taped it to my computer. I realized that when I disconnected from the meaning of my work or let it slip to the back of my mind, this note helped me avoid the dreaded "Take this job and shove it" spiral.

Maybe this sounds a little woo-woo or touchy-feely. Or it appears too simple. Just use a mental trick, and poof, your work has significance and is no longer a slog. I get it. However, your mind is incredibly powerful. Your thoughts impact how you experience your work. You can choose to experience your work positively or negatively because your beliefs and feelings are uniquely yours. No one can take them away from you, and no one can force or dictate what you must think and feel. This is your power. You can decide to perceive and experience your work as a source of meaning.

> Task, relational, and cognitive changes are all interrelated and can influence each other. For example, Celia, the Pediatric Intensive Care Unit secretary, shaped both the cognitive and task aspects of her work. She thought of herself as the "Mother Hen" of the unit and took on the additional task of purchasing drinks and snacks for the unit breakroom to support her perception of her job.

YOU TRIED TO DESIGN YOUR JOB
AND HIT A ROADBLOCK—NOW WHAT?

You took a powerful step forward to experience your work as meaningful. Then you hit a roadblock. Maybe you don't have the formal power to design your job, or your supervisor put a pin in your efforts. Maybe you *do* have the autonomy to make these shifts, but your own expectations of how you use your time hold you back. Or maybe you are constrained because you don't want to encroach on other team members. So, what can you do? Focus on the aspects of your work where you do have efficacy and control. Then be creative and adaptive.

If your position in the company affords you autonomy and formal power, this means you have influence over others. It also means you are likely responsible for the roadblocks you may experience. The first step is to own your power and responsibility. Then change your own expectations and behaviors.

For example, a director at a nonprofit, Daksh, wanted to do more student outreach, but he did not have the time to take on any additional projects. As he thought about his work, he realized while he might not be able to control all aspects of his job, he does have the power to define and guide the strategic direction of the organization. Daksh could reprioritize his team's focus areas so he and his team could spend more time on student outreach. He also recognized that everything he does each day is because he chooses to do it. The amount of time he spends on certain tasks and the prioritization of his work is decided by him. If you think about your work this way, it can help you be content with the time constraints that limit your ability to design your work and help you overcome feeling limited by your own beliefs of how you should spend your time and energy at work.

If you have limited time to design your job during your work hours, you can use your time outside of the workday. Which is what Jill did when she decided to volunteer with the Women's Connect committee in order to support, develop, and advocate for women. She is on the committee and participates in events that typically occur outside of her normal business day, either early in the morning or in the evening. There is one networking event a month and two quarterly two-day events a year. The time commitment is appropriate for her current schedule. Any more time would be prohibitive.

Now, what can you do if you work in a job where you are required to complete an assigned set of duties in a prescribed way? Maybe you are a database manager, or work in a customer call center, or do data entry. Your challenge is that you do not have the autonomy and formal power to design your job. So you focus your efforts outward. You adapt by changing others' expectations and behaviors so you can design your work. There are three ways you can do this: leverage your strengths to create opportunities, identify and reach out to people who can help you create opportunities to design your work , and/or build trust with people to create an opening to design your work.

Leverage your strengths to create opportunities.

You identified your strengths in Chapter Four in order to support the accomplishment of your company's goals. This gave you the autonomy to shape your work in a way that met both your professional and personal needs and goals. Now you can use those same strengths to provide value to your coworkers to change their opinion of you so you can create opportunities to design your work. For example, Avery, a customer service representative at a telecommunications company, studied information systems in college. She has a computer background and enjoys technology. There were technical elements of the customer service representative job that required the support of the IT department. Avery identified what she could do herself instead of the IT department and has become the go-to person to solve minor IT issues on the team. Avery proactively added tasks she enjoys, and is good at, to her job.

Reach out to people who can help.

Another strategy you can use to change others' expectations and behaviors so you can shape your work is to identify and reach out to people who can help you create opportunities to design your work. For example, Henry, a maintenance technician at a manufacturing company, wanted to improve procedures to reduce bottle cap production time. He identified a coworker in the engineering department, Jose, who could train him on the machines in the plant. Henry asked Jose about the mechanical aspects of the machines and shared with him what he observed worked and did not work on the plant floor. As a result of his association with Jose and the training he received, Henry modified the bottle cap application process and reduced production time by two minutes. He proactively added value to the company and shaped his job for more gratification.

Build trust to create an opportunity.

An additional approach you can use to change others' expectations and behaviors so you can design your work is to build trust with people to create an opening to design your work. This option will take more time, energy, and patience; however, it is very effective. For example, when Kiaan started his job at a university in the fundraising department, his job involved data entry, systems management, record keeping, email correspondence, and scheduling meetings. Kiaan wanted to help prospect and cultivate donors. He did not want to attend meetings and only take notes. Kiaan began to anticipate his manager's needs and build rapport with current donors, and demonstrated through his high-quality work that he could take on additional responsibility. His manager began to trust him and see that he was able to develop relationships and that his peers and other people in the organization trusted him. As a result, Kiaan spends most of his time now on donor cultivation, prospecting, and stewardship. He is more content and invested in his work.

Do not allow *yourself* to hold you back. Focus your time and energy where you do have control and efficiency. Then get creative and adapt. You can design your job and have more satisfaction, joy, and success.

YOU HAD A CONVERSATION
AND NOTHING HAPPENED—NOW WHAT?

Tuesday afternoon you met with your boss and discussed modifications to two of your job responsibilities. Thursday you had coffee with a team member and asked to volunteer at the after-school girls' coding program she started three months ago. Empowered and energized, you looked forward to Monday morning. That was six weeks ago. Sound familiar?

Frustrated, disappointed, angry, or perhaps nervous that you may have damaged your career, you create a story about your boss's and team member's silence and inaction. They got busy and forgot about the conversation. It's bad news so they are avoiding the conversation. They don't like change and the status quo works fine for them. It's a political quagmire that requires extra energy, time, documentation, and/or political capital. They are lazy and do not want to go to the effort to advocate on your behalf. It could be any, all, or a combination of these reasons. The problem is that you don't know. You are caught in a vicious and unproductive cycle of conjecture, fabrication, and fantasy.

To get what you asked for, you must know the specific cause of the unresponsiveness. And the only way to find out is to have a follow-up conversation. Before you schedule the conversation, you need to be clear on why your request matters to you.

- What was the catalyst for your ask? What's at stake if you don't receive what you asked for?

- How will what you asked for constructively impact you, your career, your team, and the company?

- What is the feeling that drove your ask?

- What do you *really* want?

I want to give you examples to help you brainstorm your answers to these questions. However, sometimes my clients get stuck on my suggestions or ideas and think that these are the only way to solve a challenge. Then they try to fit their life and their unique situation to my example. So I am not going to give you examples. I don't want you to take other people's stories and make them fit your situation. Why? Because this is personal. You are on Chapter Seven. If you have been doing the exercises and reflection activities in this book, you've got this. I know you can do it. I am cheering you on.

Invest the time to answer each question. Your answers help you move through any residual negativity, anger, or frustration back to the confident, positive, empowered person who asked for what you needed and wanted. Now you are ready to have the follow-up conversation.

The follow-up conversation will include three parts: state the facts of the situation, share your story about the facts, and ask for your manager's perspective.

Start the Conversation with the Facts

You start the conversation with the facts, because if you begin by sharing your feelings or stories, the other person may not understand what you're talking about or may become defensive or angry and withdraw from the conversation. For example, if you tell a friend that she can't be trusted (your story) and offer no further explanation, she isn't sure why you drew this undesirable conclusion. Then, since she's been accused of being untrustworthy, she will become defensive and get angry. The original facts may never even make it into the conversation.

Feelings and stories often keep you from the facts. Facts clarify the topic of conversation, and they are more persuasive and less controversial than stories. When you need to have a difficult conversation or share something that the other person might resist, it is more effective to share the facts behind the story before you share your story.

However, when we are emotionally charged, it can be easy to confuse facts with stories. A fact is an actual occurrence. It is something that can be proved through observation or measurement. Facts are what you saw and heard. For example, you met with Selena, your manager, on Tuesday, June 2. It is now Tuesday, July 7, five weeks since your conversation. You have not received an email or a phone call or had the in-person conversation you were promised about the two modifications to your job responsibilities. Based on these facts you would begin the conversation, "Selena, we met on Tuesday, June 2, and I asked you to modify two of my job responsibilities. It has been five weeks since that meeting, and I have not received any additional information or communication from you."

Here are a few additional phrases you can use to make your points.

- "I saw ..."
- "I noticed that ..."
- "The last three times we talked about this ..."

- "I was expecting you to be here at 7:00 a.m., and it's now 7:30 a.m. . . ."

Sometimes the stories we tell ourselves about our boss's inaction hinder our progress. Again, a story is a judgment, conclusion, or attribution you make from the facts. A judgment is used to determine whether facts are good or bad. You draw conclusions to fit elements of your story together. And you use attributions to explain why people do what they do. For example, you conclude that you have not heard from your boss Selena because she is lazy. She does not want to spend the time or the effort to advocate on your behalf. The problem with our stories is that they can be insulting or harsh or can include unattractive assumptions about another person's behavior. If you shared these suppositions with other person, it's only natural that the person would feel hurt or insulted. In contrast, when you share only what you've seen and heard, others are less likely to be offended. Start your conversation with the facts.

Share Your Story About the Facts

Of course, facts by themselves don't always show the whole picture, which is why the second part of the conversation is where you share your story about the facts. Your story addresses why the facts matter to you. It describes *your* experience of the facts. When you share your story, it is imperative that you carefully choose your words and phrases. Avoid absolutes such as "must," "have to," or "the fact of the matter is . . ." You do not want to jeopardize the goal of the conversation, which is to understand the reason why no action was taken on your request.

Use one of the phrases below to avoid triggering an angry or defensive response:

- "I'm starting to think . . ."
- "The story I'm telling myself is . . ."[8]
- "It seems to me that . . ."
- "I'm wondering if . . ."

For example, "I'm starting to think that it requires a lot of your time and energy to navigate human resources and the politics of modifying two of my job responsibilities."

Sometimes when I do this exercise with my clients, they are concerned they will do all the talking and the conversation will last too long. Don't worry. This is a quick process. It takes approximately three to four minutes to state the facts and share your story. These are succinct statements that establish the context of the conversation.

Use an open-ended question or one of the following questions:

- "What am I missing?"
- "Can you help me better understand what happened?"
- "How do you see it?"
- "What's your perspective?"

Invite Your Manager's Perspective

Now you are ready for the final step in the process, to invite your manager into the conversation and ask for their perspective. Once you've delivered the facts and your story, pause and listen carefully to your manager's response. When you know the specific reason why no action has been taken on your request, you can look for and find a mutually beneficial solution with your manager.

However, what do you do if your manager does not offer their perspective or provide any additional information? What if they become angry or withdraw from the conversation? When someone has a reaction like this, it's not because of *what* you are saying; it's because of *why* they think you're having the conversation.[9] If they think your purpose is to blame, shame, or win, then they are going to either get angry or withdraw and avoid any additional interaction with you. For example, if Selena assumes the intent of your conversation is to tell her that you believe she is a lazy, ineffective, self-centered manager who does not care about you or your professional fulfillment, she will feel threatened and inadequate and exit the conversation.

If a conversation moves in this direction, restart it by first clarifying any misunderstandings that may have led your manager to confuse why you are having this conversation. When your manager knows that your intent is positive, they don't worry that you are trying to force a solution, and they will be more willing to listen and hear your potentially negative or painful content. Explain your intent. Use a phrase that begins with "What," such as "What I was trying to say" or "What I meant was." Or "Selena, what I was trying to say is that working with human resources right now to approve modifying my job responsibilities is probably a challenge because of the time and energy required to launch our new product. I know you are committed to both me and the success of our new product."

Once your manager realizes the conversation is not a personal attack and your intent is positive, the next step is to establish a shared goal that benefits both of you. You might say to Selena, "Let's look at what is preventing us from moving forward and brainstorm ideas that will work for both of us." Be open, receptive, and creative. And if you and your manager have different goals, think about how you can combine them so that you both get what you want and need. For example, if Selena needs to focus her time on the new product launch and you want to modify your job responsibilities, you could offer to meet with human resources and collect the required documentation and then help Selena complete the process. In this instance you both get what you want and need.

It may make you feel frustrated, demoralized, or upset to ask for what you want and need and be met with silence and inaction. When this occurs, don't languish in silence and wish, hope, or pray for something to change. You are not helpless. Step up again and ask for a follow-up conversation. Uncover the reason for the inaction, and then work together to find a mutually beneficial resolution.

Remember, the meaning, value, and purpose of work is defined by you. It is uniquely yours. You can design your work to derive more value and fulfillment when you modify the task, relational, and cognitive aspects of your job. And when you hit a roadblock, you have the power to step up and have a conversation to uncover what is actually standing between you and your professional dreams.

You did it! You have turned your job into your dream job. Congratulations!

Now, it's time for us to celebrate you and your new life.

CONCLUSION

You Did and You Will

*What matters isn't that we attain perfection, but that again
and again with humility and faith, we reach.*

Cheryl Strayed

Heart racing, I walked into the conference room with what felt like a too-big smile on my face. It had only been four weeks since I'd graduated from college and started my career at a Fortune 100 company in an intensive leadership development program. Now here I was at 23 years old about to have lunch with the CEO and his entire leadership team. I could not believe that I was going to meet and spend time with the leaders I aspired to be.

As I surveyed the room, I glanced at the woman seated at the end of the long conference table. Her face was drawn and tight, and there were dark circles under her eyes that her makeup could not conceal. She had the gray pallor of someone who had been sick for a long time. Her shoulders were hunched up almost touching her ears. However, it was her eyes that were the most disturbing. It was as if someone had turned off the lights to her soul.

I quickly looked away and sat in my seat. The CEO welcomed us and introduced each person on his executive team. When he got to the woman at the end of the table, he said, "This is my chief human resources officer." I was stunned and confused. The woman with the pinched face and sad eyes was responsible for all 27,000 of us?

She stood up and talked about her "people" strategy, employee engagement, and how to develop the next generation of leaders: me and my colleagues in this room. With each word she spoke, she seemed more and more unhappy, even miserable, as though the life had been sucked out of her—burned out, overwhelmed, demotivated, and unfulfilled.

Is this what success looks like?

Not anymore.

And never again because you are different now.

You have turned your job into your dream job.

When you turned to page 1 in this book, you probably could not even imagine the scope of the possibilities that existed for you. Was it possible to no longer dread Monday mornings or count down the days to the weekend? Could you be fulfilled, content, gratified, and engaged at work? Could you make a living *and* a life? Was it even conceivable to have a dream job?

What you know now is yes! Maybe even a "Hell yes!"

Because *you* are the catalyst that changed your professional life.

The give-and-take of the employer-employee social contract, is the new dynamic of your relationship with your employer. The skills, experiences, and abilities that you contribute are vital and meaningful to your employer. They are the engine that fuels your organization's growth. When you join a company, you do not abdicate your personal power. Neither your boss nor your company has all the power in the relationship. You have an equal and powerful voice. You chose to follow the path to own, love, and make your job work for you.

OWN IT

Your bold, courageous decision to walk through Door Number Four, the door of possibility and choice, began your transformational journey. Your first stop—to own it. To know that you are capable, competent, significant, and a valued team member and that you make a difference in your company. You embraced a growth mindset, asked for feedback, and used the SEE feedback model—specific, example, explain—to create more opportunities for positive, successful work experiences. The brain's "negativity bias" did not stop you. Simple, yet powerful, tools enabled you to liberate yourself from the "Work sucks" refrain. And you recognized and asked for the acknowledgment and praise you need to receive for your efforts.

You embraced your strengths as your professional gold in the employer-employee social contract because they enable you to have more control and choice over what you work on and how you work. You aligned your strengths to your company's goals so you could shape your work in a way that met both your professional and personal needs and ambitions. You identified what you wanted from the relationship with your employer and asked for it.

You owned it!

LOVE IT

It was now time to rekindle the passion and joy in your work. This required that you acquire new capabilities and knowledge and find ways to advance in your career. So you assessed your current skills and expertise to create your Abilities Opportunity Map—your personalized professional development plan. You chose to invest in yourself. An investment that has paid off—in increased confidence, additional opportunities for a promotion or a raise, enhanced value to your team and company, and more time and energy for the people, hobbies, and projects that interest you.

Your focus then shifted to your teammates, boss, and colleagues because positive relationships in the workplace are essential for your contentment and professional success. The Platinum Rule is now the compass you use anytime you connect and collaborate with others so you can foster mutual respect and understanding. SCARF threats no longer undermine your interactions with other people in your company, and you recognize when you have climbed up the Ladder of Inference. You experience more positive social interactions and build stronger relationships because you do not get stuck on the Ladder of Inference unable to climb down.

You now love it!

MAKE IT WORK

The final stop on your transformational journey to turn any job into your dream job was to make your job work for you. This is where you went deeper to find *your* meaning in your work. You recognized that the value and importance of your work is defined by you. It is personal. Meaning is what you bring to the table. It is uniquely yours. No one can define it for you. You embraced your power to design your work to be more significant, purposeful, and valuable to you. You made behavioral changes to your tasks or to your professional relationships, or you made proactive psychological changes to your perceptions of your job. And you if you hit a roadblock when you attempted to redesign your work, you took another approach or had another conversation with your manager. At no point did you give up on your dream.

You made it work!

• • •

At every step along the journey, you have realized that small, incremental shifts are powerful and life changing. I am certain that you have the skills, tools, and drive to take any job and own it, love it, and make it work for you. The fact that you have achieved *all* of this makes you a champion in my mind. You have the courage to face your fears, the detractors, and the corporate politics that come your way. You have the persistence to do the hard work. You have unshakable commitment to your goals and dreams.

There are infinite strategies, tools, and approaches to address the Sunday night scaries, Monday morning blues, and how work sucks—the rest is up to you. As long as you know the steps along the journey to find your professional bliss, I know you will find your way. I know that any job can be your dream job.

I hope that the knowledge you have gained in this book becomes your most reliable map to unleash your professional goals and dreams and that it serves you for the rest of your career.

I am proud of you. I am honored and humbled that you allowed me to be a part of your journey. Thank you.

ACCELERATION GUIDE

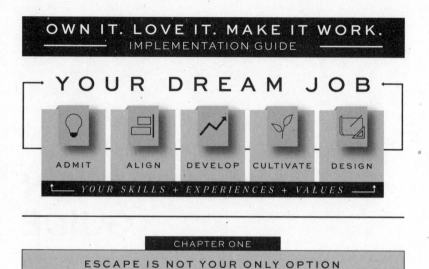

YOUR DREAM JOB

ADMIT · ALIGN · DEVELOP · CULTIVATE · DESIGN

YOUR SKILLS + EXPERIENCES + VALUES

CHAPTER ONE

ESCAPE IS NOT YOUR ONLY OPTION

It is time to own your power in the relationship with your employer so you can turn your current job into your dream job. *You can and are the catalyst for change in your life.*

IMPLEMENTATION STEP:

 Email carson@carsontate.com—"I chose to make a living and be happy."

CHAPTER TWO

USE YOUR FEAR & EMBRACE YOUR SUPERPOWERS

Fear compels us to get clear on what matters. Use it as a catalyst for action. Everything you need is inside of you right now to turn an unfulfilling, unhappy work life into a vibrant, significant, joyful one.

Allow your superpowers—choice and control—to shine brightly so you can create the job of your dreams.

NAME AND CLAIM YOUR FEARS

IMPLEMENTATION STEPS:

- [ ] Complete the list of your fears exercise on page 21.
- [ ] Complete your job assessment on page 22.
- [ ] Complete the reflection questions for each "false" answer on pages 22–23.

YOUR SUPERPOWERS: CHOICE AND CONTROL

IMPLEMENTATION STEP:

- [ ] Complete reflection questions to unlock your superpowers on pages 32–34.

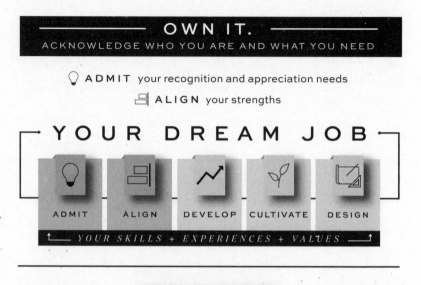

OWN IT.
ACKNOWLEDGE WHO YOU ARE AND WHAT YOU NEED

ADMIT your recognition and appreciation needs
ALIGN your strengths

YOUR DREAM JOB

| ADMIT | ALIGN | DEVELOP | CULTIVATE | DESIGN |

YOUR SKILLS + EXPERIENCES + VALUES

CHAPTER THREE

ADMIT YOUR RECOGNITION AND APPRECIATION NEEDS

Acknowledge, identify, and ask for the recognition and appreciation due to you in exchange for your contributions so you can turn your current job into your dream job.

CULTIVATE POSITIVE SELF-ESTEEM AT WORK THROUGH FEEDBACK

IMPLEMENTATION STEP:

☐ Identify one opportunity to proactively ask for feedback and use the SEE framework on page 46.

OVERRIDE YOUR BRAIN'S "NEGATIVITY BIAS"

IMPLEMENTATION STEP:

☐ Implement one of the following strategies on pages 50–54:

- Rehearse good news and share it.
- Share two roses and a thorn.
- Break the cycle.
- Feed the positive.

- Feed the positive.
- Keep a report card on your best efforts.
- Notice when you're negative.
- Focus on solving problems.

TAKE OWNERSHIP FOR YOUR RECOGNITION NEEDS

IMPLEMENTATION STEPS:

☐ Complete the reflection questions on page 56 to identify how you want to be recognized and praised for your contributions.

☐ Schedule the meeting with your manager to ask for the acknowledgment and affirmation you need.

☐ Rehearse the conversation you will have with your manager with a friend or colleague.

☐ Meet with your manager and ask for the acknowledgment and affirmation you need.

SHOW ME THE MONEY

IMPLEMENTATION STEPS:

☐ Document your track record of exemplary performance.

☐ Schedule a meeting with your manager to solicit specific feedback on how you can enhance your performance and position yourself for your next role.

☐ Proactively communicate your accomplishments and how you have contributed to the success of the business to your manager.

☐ Research your market value.

☐ Script the conversation you will have with your manager to ask for a raise.

☐ Practice the conversation you will have with your manager to ask for a raise.

CHAPTER FOUR

⊟| ALIGN YOUR STRENGTHS

Your strengths are those activities that you are good at, you can't not do them, you seek out opportunities to develop them, and you need to do them.

Your strengths make you feel gratified and fulfilled. They are your professional gold.

Align your strengths to support the accomplishment of the company's goals so you can design your work in a way that meets both your professional and personal needs and goals.

EXCAVATE YOUR STRENGTHS

→ IMPLEMENTATION STEPS: ←

- ☐ Decide if you will use reflection journaling, performance reviews/360 feedback reports, or a calendar and task list analysis to complete your strengths list.

- ☐ Reflection Journaling: For one week answer the questions on page 73.

- ☐ Reflection Journaling: Review your answers to the reflection questions and identify the patterns or themes that emerged.

- ☐ Reflection Journaling: List at least three strengths.

- ☐ Performance Reviews/360 Feedback Reports: Complete the analysis of your reviews by following the steps on pages 74–75.

- ☐ Performance Reviews/360 Feedback Reports: Review your list of statements and identify your core theme.

- ☐ Performance Reviews/360 Feedback Reports: List at least three strengths.

- ☐ Calendar and Task List Analysis: For one work week complete steps one and two on pages 76–77.

- ☐ Calendar and Task List Analysis: At the end of the workweek complete step three on page 77.

- ☐ Calendar and Task List Analysis: Review your list of ranked activities and answer the questions on page 77 for your top three activities.

- ☐ Calendar and Task List Analysis: List at least three strengths and write your strengths statement.

ALIGN YOUR STRENGTHS TO YOUR ORGANIZATION'S GOALS

IMPLEMENTATION STEPS:

☐ Review your company's strategic plan.

☐ Review your team's goals.

☐ Identify how your top three strengths support the obtainment of any, all or some of the goals by answering the questions on page 81.

☐ Document your track record of efficacious alignment between your strengths, the company's and team's goals by answering the quesions on page 82.

☐ Brainstorm additional ways you can deploy your strengths to support your company's and team's goals by answering the questions on page 82.

☐ List the activities you loathe doing on one of four lists—stop, reduce, partner, or reframe.

☐ Complete the stop step on page 83.

☐ Complete the reduce step on page 83.

☐ Complete the partner step on pages 83–84.

☐ Complete the reframe step on page 84.

☐ Take the action step(s) you identified for the stop step.

☐ Take the action step(s) you identified for the reduce step.

☐ Take the action step(s) you identified for the partner step.

☐ Take the action step(s) you identified for the reframe step.

☐ Schedule a meeting with your manager to discuss your strengths, how they have supported and enabled the company's and team's attainment of its goals, and your ideas to spend more time working from your strengths.

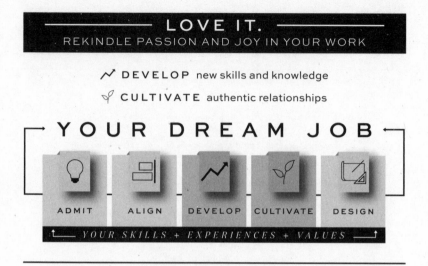

LOVE IT.
REKINDLE PASSION AND JOY IN YOUR WORK

〆 **DEVELOP** new skills and knowledge

❦ **CULTIVATE** authentic relationships

YOUR DREAM JOB

ADMIT · ALIGN · DEVELOP · CULTIVATE · DESIGN

YOUR SKILLS + EXPERIENCES + VALUES

CHAPTER FIVE
〆 DEVELOP NEW SKILLS AND KNOWLEDGE

Professional growth and development enable you to stay agile, excited, passionate, and engaged in your job.

Assess your current skills and knowledge to create your professional development plan.

Choose to invest in yourself.

CREATE YOUR ABILITIES OPPORTUNITY MAP
→ IMPLEMENTATION STEPS: ←

☐ Complete the skills assessment on page 94.

☐ For each question you marked true, complete the steps beneath each question beginning on page 97.

☐ Decide the type of skill set—soft, hard, or hybrid—you need to develop by completing the chart on page 101.

☐ List the top three skills you want to develop.

IDENTIFY HOW YOU WILL ACQUIRE YOUR NEW SKILLS AND KNOWLEDGE

→ IMPLEMENTATION STEPS: ←

☐ List how you will acquire the new capability or knowledge for each of the top three skills you want to develop.

☐ Assess the professional development opportunity you identified to develop your new skill by answering the quesions on pages 113–114.

☐ Select the professional development opportunity based on your assessment.

CHAPTER SIX

CULTIVATE AUTHENTIC RELATIONSHIPS

Positive relationships are essential for our well-being and productivity.

Identify where you undermine your efforts at connection and collaboration and develop new approaches and strategies so you can experience more positive social interactions and build stronger relationships.

USE THE PLATINUM RULE TO FOSTER MUTUAL RESPECT AND UNDERSTANDING

→ IMPLEMENTATION STEPS: ←

- [ ] Identify your work style. Take the assessment at www.workingsimply.com/productivity-purchase.
- [ ] Identify the work style of your manager and/or colleagues using the descriptions on pages 122 and 124.

DISCOVER HOW YOU UNCONSCIOUSLY UNDERMINE YOUR RELATIONSHIPS

→ IMPLEMENTATION STEPS: ←

- [ ] Identify your primary SCARF threat using the descriptions on pages 130–132 and the reflection questions on page 134.
- [ ] Identify a specific action step you can take to minimize a status threat to you and to a teammate.
- [ ] Identify a specific action step you can take to minimize a certainty threat to you and to a teammate.
- [ ] Identify a specific action step you can take to minimize an autonomy threat to you and to a teammate.
- [ ] Identify a specific action step you can take to minimize a relatedness threat to you and to a teammate.
- [ ] Identify a specific action step you can take to minimize a fairness threat to you and to a teammate.

STOP MAKING NEGATIVE ASSUMPTIONS ABOUT YOUR COLLEAGUE'S BEHAVIOR

→ IMPLEMENTATION STEP: ←

- [ ] Get off the Ladder of Interference:

- Cite what you heard or saw.
- Assume and grant honorable intentions.
- Ask for what you missed.
- Compare perceptions and stories so you can check your confirmation bias.
- Listen. Suggest an action step focused on mutual shared interests.

MAKE IT WORK.
MAKE YOUR JOB WORK FOR YOU

DESIGN your work to find *your* meaning

YOUR DREAM JOB

| ADMIT | ALIGN | DEVELOP | CULTIVATE | DESIGN |

YOUR SKILLS + EXPERIENCES + VALUES

CHAPTER SEVEN

DESIGN YOUR WORK TO FIND YOUR MEANING

The value and importance of your work is defined by you. Meaning is not controlled by what happens in your life. It is made by your interpretation of the events in your life.

It is impossible to provide a universal, one-size-fits-all definition of meaningful work. It is subjective.

Meaning is what you bring to the table. No one can define it for you.

DESIGN YOUR WORK FOR MORE MEANING

→ IMPLEMENTATION STEPS: ←

☐ Decide which area you want to focus on to design your work: task, relational, or cognitive boundaries.

☐ Task: Identify the job duty you can modify or responsibility you can add to your current role by answering the questions on page 160.

☐ Task: Modify your job responsibility.

☐ Task: Schedule a meeting with your manager if approval is required to modify your job responsibility.

☐ Relational: Complete the modify a professional relationship exercise on pages 162–164.

☐ Relational: Complete two action steps you identified in the modify a professional relationship exercise.

☐ Relational: Complete two action steps you identified in the modify a professional relationship exercise.

☐ Relational: Identify a passion, special interest, experience, or skill you want to develop.

☐ Relational: Research and identify the person or people who can help you.

☐ Relational: Schedule a meeting with the person or people who can help you.

☐ Cognitive: List all your job accountabilities.

☐ Cognitive: Ask yourself "So, what?" for each of your job accountabilities.

☐ Cognitive: Review your "So, what?" answers and answer the questions on page 168.

☐ Cognitive: Describe the central objective of your work.

☐ Cognitive: Write a meaning statement for your work.

☐ Post your meaning statement where you can see it.

ABILITIES OPPORTUNITY MAP

ABILITIES OPPORTUNITY MAP

YOUR DREAM JOB

| ADMIT | ALIGN | DEVELOP | CULTIVATE | DESIGN |

YOUR SKILLS + EXPERIENCES + VALUES

SOFT SKILLS	HARD SKILLS	HYBRID SKILLS

MY TOP THREE SKILLS TO DEVELOP

SKILLS TO DEVELOP	SKILL TYPE	HOW?

©2020 WORKING SIMPLY, INC

GROW YOUR CAREER

In Chapter Five you identified the new abilities and knowledge you wanted to acquire and developed your personal professional development plan, your Abilities Opportunity Map. Now you may be thinking, "What about my current skills, expertise, and talents? How can I use these to progress in my career and increase my professional opportunities?" These can be used to GROW Your Career, which is based on the acronym GROW:

Get clear.

Recognize your results.

Own your impact.

Where and what else?

Follow the four steps below to create a plan to leverage your current skills, expertise, and talents so you can expand your professional opportunities and use your talents to advance your career.

You will complete the four GROW steps for each of your jobs and volunteer positions.

STEP 1: GET CLEAR

If you are not clear on the experiences and capabilities you possess, it is difficult to imagine how you can use them differently to expand and advance your career.

Let's do a Career + Life Walk. It is a simple, yet powerful, process that enables you to methodically assess each professional role and position throughout your career history, as well as your volunteer service. It is important to include your volunteer service because there may be experiences and aptitudes you gained through volunteering that can be valuable to you now.

You'll need a few things to complete your Career + Life Walk:

- Your résumé

- Your curriculum vitae

- Your LinkedIn profile bio

- Your bio on your company's website

- Any other documentation that includes your entire career history and complete list of your volunteer service

It is important that you have your *entire* career history because you want a complete inventory of your experiences and expertise.

1. Start with your first job and answer the three questions below:

   - **What was your specific role?**
     For example, operations manager for a conference center.

   - **What were you responsible for?**
     For example, overseeing and managing the staff and operations for six departments including Guest Services, Human Resources, Event Planning and Programs, Housekeeping, Kitchen, and Facilities and Maintenance.

   - **What did you *do*?**
     Focus on the actions you performed as part of your responsibilities. These are the physical, tangible steps you performed. Here's a hint: all actions start with an action verb. For example, *set*, *met*, *develop*, *analyze*, *coach*, or *explain*. Remember, your goal is to get clear. Remove any abstractions and any consultant or MBA school jargon and assumptions.

     For example, what did you do to manage the staff? Set customer service rating goals for each team member. Met with each team member once a month to review the member's customer service rating report. Developed a performance improvement plan for each team member to increase individual customer service ratings to five stars.

2. Answer all three questions for each of your job and volunteer positions.

3. Review your responses to the third question, "What did you do?," and identify the following:

- Any actions you had forgotten about
- Themes or clusters of actions that you do not use in your current role
- Actions that intellectually stimulated, challenged, or motivated you

You will come back to the answers to these questions in the last step, "Where and What Else?"

STEP 2: RECOGNIZE YOUR RESULTS

Your results are the benefit you bring to an individual, a team, and/or a company. This is important in the employer-employee social contract of give-and-take because this is what you give to an organization. To better use your existing skills, experiences, and talents, it is imperative that you know and can articulate the advantage of each of these for your manager, team, and company.

1. Start with your first job and answer the three questions below:

   - **What were my quantitative outcomes? So what?** Quantitative results can be counted, measured, and expressed with numbers. Specifically identify each quantitative outcome, and then ask yourself the "So what?" question. Numbers without context allow other people to tell your story. You need to tell your own story and clearly communicate the value of the outcome you achieved.

For example, you increased supplier diversity by 35 percent. So what? This promoted innovation in your company through the introduction of new products, services, and solutions. It provided multiple channels to source goods and services, and it drove competition (on price and service levels) between your company's existing and potential vendors.

- **What were my qualitative results?**

  Qualitative results are descriptive and conceptual. They can be categorized based on traits and characteristics.

  For example, a member of your team enhanced their communication skills to be more succinct, precise, and factual in their presentations to your customers.

- **What was my overall impact in the role?**

  When I started in this position, our revenue was _____, our customer service ratings were _____, the team's engagement level was _____, the team's internal reputation was _____, and the team's contributions to the company were _____.

  If some of the above items are not relevant to you and your position, replace them with what is applicable for you.

  When you left this role, what was different in each of the above categories or the categories you added?

2. Answer all three questions for each of your job and volunteer positions.

STEP 3: OWN YOUR IMPACT

In each of your professional and volunteer positions, you made an impact. Your customers, your team, the company, the community, or an individual was changed because of you and your work. For example, maybe your department had the highest customer service ratings in the company, or maybe the high school student you mentored was the first member of their family to go to college.

1. Read the results you achieved and pause for three seconds.

2. Acknowledge yourself and your contributions.

    In our always-on, fast-paced, push-and-strive-to-achieve-more world, we rarely stop, notice, and celebrate what we did and the impact we made in and for the world. Stop. Pause. Celebrate. You obtained that result. Own it!

3. Identify the feeling you experienced when you read your results.

    You may be tempted to skip this step because it appears too soft, woo-woo, or insignificant. I get it. However, there are positive feelings associated with each of your results. Positive feelings are one of the five elements that help people reach a life of fulfillment and meaning according to Martin Seligman, one of the founders of positive psychology.[1] So, what do you feel when you read your results? Joy? Hope? Confidence? Contentment? Enthusiasm? Pride? Satisfaction? You are on a transformational journey to find more happiness and fulfillment at work. Feel the feelings. Let them move through your body. Now, don't you want to feel those feelings again? Or more of them?

STEP 4: WHERE AND WHAT ELSE?

Ask yourself two questions:

1. Where else can you use the actions you identified in the "Get Clear" step that intellectually stimulated, challenged, and motivated you, *and* that generated positive emotions from the results you achieved?

    Think about how you can use your actions to increase the scope of your current responsibilities.

    - What do you want to do more of in your current role?

    - How do your results demonstrate that you can expand the scope of your responsibilities and take on a new project or assignment?

    - Where can you volunteer for a company-wide project or committee that would enable you to use the actions you identified?

2. What else can these actions be used for?

    Often my coaching clients get stuck thinking that they can only use their expertise in one way. This one-track thinking limits your possibilities. Our goal is to expand your opportunities and use your talents to advance your career.

    For example, you developed a performance improvement plan for each member of your team. The results? A 40 percent increase in five-star ratings across the team, and your company won a customer service award at your industry's national conference. You felt pride and joy in these results. So, what else can you do with the action "developed a performance improvement plan"? You could develop a performance improvement plan for any person, project, or company-wide initiative that is underperforming. Could you stretch and put together a plan to launch a new project? Could you design a training program to improve customer service? Be creative and don't limit yourself or your possibilities

It can be hard to brainstorm alone. Ask a coworker, mentor, friend, or significant other to help you dream, ideate, and explore possibilities.

WORKPLACE DISCRIMINATION RESOURCE GUIDE

I conducted an interview with Tom Wilinsky, an attorney with more than 25 years' experience in employment law in New York and New Jersey, to understand workplace discrimination and what you can do if you experience discrimination in your workplace.

1. **What is the legal definition of discrimination?**
   Discrimination is treating someone in a way that's different from other people because that person is included in a class that the law considers "protected," meaning historically marginalized, or entitled to equal treatment but often treated differently based on an improper characteristic.

The protected classes are the following:

- Gender

- Race/color

- Ethnicity

- Religion

- Sexuality in some states

- Pregnancy

- Disability

- Age

Discrimination based on your looks, the sound of your voice, your personality, or your economic class does not count. It must fall into one of the above categories.

2. **What is an example of different treatment?**
   For example, we're firing you because you're X. We're promoting someone else because he's white and male, but we're not promoting you because you're nonwhite and you're female. We're not hiring you because you're not the race or ethnicity we like.

3. **Is sexual harassment a form of discrimination?**
   Yes. For example, "I will not promote you unless you engage in sexual activities with me."

   This is sexual harassment, a form of discrimination, which is illegal.

4. **Are there any other forms of discrimination?**
   Yes. Discrimination can also occur in the form of different wages, bonuses, or any other of the privileges that you

receive that you can quantify at work, like insurance coverage or use of particular services, because you fall into one of the protected categories.

It can also be more subtle. For example, a female litigation attorney was on an all-male litigation team. In the litigation strategy planning meeting, she shared a thought about their approach and the man leading the meeting turned to another man at the meeting and said, "Did you see the game last night?" There was no response, nor acknowledgment of her statement. She was essentially cut out of the meeting. That is discriminatory. It's not necessarily enough for a legal claim for compensation, but it's one of the typical ways that discrimination occurs in the workplace.

5. **What is a hostile workplace environment? How does this relate to workplace discrimination?**
   A hostile workplace environment is not just an environment where you are treated poorly. A mean boss or vicious colleague doesn't count. It's an environment that is so infected with discriminatory acts that it makes it impossible for you to do your job. For example, if you're a woman in a largely male workplace and there are constant jokes about sex or there is sexually explicit material throughout the office, you may find it impossible to do your job. Because this workplace is so infested with offensive sex talk and material to the point at which you can't get your work done, it's considered a hostile work environment.

6. **What are my options if I am being discriminated in my workplace?**

   a. **Keep a record of the behavior.**

   I always tell a client to write down the specific behavior, the date, and who is doing it. After a couple of times, you may notice a trend or pattern and may want to do something about it.

   b. **Talk to a trusted colleague, mentor, or manager in your workplace.**

   If you have a good relationship with someone in the workplace, it's usually helpful to get a second opinion on the suspected discrimination, particularly if that person is in the same class as you are. For example, if you're a woman in a largely male workplace and you have a mentor who's a woman, it's often helpful to talk to her about the behavior. This is a casual, less risky means to evaluate the behavior.

   Be aware that if you do talk to a colleague, mentor, or manager about suspected discrimination, your conversation may get around the office in an uncontrolled way. It is also hard to know whether your colleague will handle it in a way that benefits you.

   c. **Contact your human resources department.**

   Human resources departments often have policies and procedures in place to resolve reports of discrimination. There is a risk that your conversation will not be kept confidential.

   Additionally, I have had clients who pursued this option and were subsequently treated as a problem employee and the complaint was not resolved. If the evidence is clear and human resources either does nothing and continues to allow the employee to be subject to discrimination or makes it worse, than HR's actions are illegal. If the situation is less clear, such as where the evidence isn't there, but the employee is certain they have been victimized, HR's abilities may be limited and it's not necessarily illegal.

Some employers have systems set up for mediation or group resolution. For example, human resources may agree to moderate a conversation between you and someone who has acted in a discriminatory manner in an attempt to find a resolution that is agreeable to both parties. Such a conversation may lead to sensitivity training for the offending person and/or reassignment for the victim.

d. **Contact your company's employee assistance program.**
An employee assistance program (EAP) is a voluntary, work-based *program* that offers free and confidential assessments, short-term counseling, referrals, and follow-up services to employees who have personal and/or work-related problems. There is no charge to an employee for use of this service, as it is paid for by the employer.

This service is confidential.

e. **Contact the Equal Employment Opportunity Commission.**
The Equal Employment Opportunity Commission (EEOC) is the federal governmental agency that

handles employment discrimination. Most states and cities also have an agency that functions like the EEOC, and the state and city agencies work in tandem with the federal agency.

The EEOC provides information and has procedures for reporting a discrimination claim. You have three options for reporting a discrimination claim: online, in person, or via telephone. Reporting your claim to the EEOC is a significant step because you are starting a legal process. When you go to the EEOC with a claim, the agency will contact the employer, and the employer has the right to say that there has been no discrimination for various reasons.

If you report a claim to the EEOC or a state or local agency, it will take your formal complaint and commence an investigation. This will be either an extensive or a minor investigation. Based on the findings of the investigation, one of the following will happen:

- The EEOC will tell you that you have probable cause to file a claim for discrimination and that it will not handle it. Note: This is the most frequent response from the EEOC, and it is called a right-to-sue letter. You take the letter and go to a federal or state court and pursue the claim yourself. You would incur the legal fees if you chose this option.

- The EEOC will tell you that it is going to start a formal investigation. If this happens, the EEOC believes your claim sufficiently enough to conduct an investigation of your employer.

- The EEOC will tell you that this does not appear to be discrimination and that it will not pursue it or give you a right-to-sue letter. This does not mean you cannot start a lawsuit, but it does mean that the EEOC or state agency did not find sufficient evidence of discrimination to be confident in your claim.

f. **Contact an employment attorney.**
There are employment attorneys in every state who advertise and will often offer free consultations. The employment attorneys may be of varying quality, but you have nothing to lose, and if you consult an attorney, it's confidential. The attorney is obliged to maintain the attorney-client privilege that ensures your confidentiality.

One option you have with an attorney is for the attorney to send a letter, threatening to sue and laying out the claims to your employer. If successful, you can then enter into a confidential agreement with your employer and you are not in a public database. If you do decide to leave your employer, your attorney can help you agree on a script for your reference from your employer. The standard reference statement is "We employed X in the following position(s) and we confirm that X worked from this date to that date."

g. **Go directly to a state court and sue for discrimination.**
In many states, you can go straight to a state court and sue for discrimination without going to the EEOC or the state or local version of the EEOC. If you choose this option, you are immediately commencing a

lawsuit against your employer. This is an adversarial process, and if you're still in the workplace, that can be very uncomfortable. Additionally, the lawsuit is now public record. It states that you made a discrimination claim against your employer and usually contains the employer's denial. If employers do a background check prior to employment, this will show up in the report.

Alternatively, many employers have employees sign a contract agreeing to arbitrate any claims they have, including discrimination claims. This would prevent you from going to court but would not prevent you from bringing a claim, with or without an attorney, in an arbitration forum.

7. **Are there any other options or advice you give people when they are experiencing discrimination, but they are in a position where they need the job to care for their family or they want to stay with their employer?**
I always tell people, "Your best revenge is your next job." Keep your eyes and ears open for other positions within your company. Is there an opportunity within another group or with another manager? Sometimes it is just one person who has a grudge or who is engaging in discriminatory behavior. For example, I had a client who was a salesperson who placed cosmetics in department stores. A new manager was hired for her team, and he said, "I don't like ugly people. I don't like fat people. I don't like older people. I want only young, beautiful people manning these cosmetic counters." My client was concerned that

her new boss was setting her and her colleagues up to be fired. Since she had been at the company longer than her boss, she was able to go to someone else who worked at the company in a different department and say, "I'm concerned that this is going on." She was offered a position in another department, and her boss was eventually fired.

Build relationships and network within your industry so you can find a new job outside of your company. If you do decide to leave your employer, you can decide once you have left if you want to sue your previous employer for discrimination.

THOMAS B. WILINSKY, ESQ.

Biancone & Wilinsky, LLP

www.bianconeandwilinsky.com

Bar Admissions

New York, 1992

New Jersey, 1998

Education

- New York University School of Law, New York, New York
  - J.D. – 1991
- New York University, Graduate School of Arts & Sciences, New York, New York
  - M.A. – 1988
- Connecticut College, New London, Connecticut
  - B.A. – 1986

Thomas B. Wilinsky has practiced law for more than twenty-five years. Mr. Wilinsky has a Bachelor's Degree, Magna Cum Laude, in Economics from Connecticut College, where he a was member of the Phi Beta Kappa Honor Society, and a Master of Arts Degree in Liberal Studies from New York University. Prior to attending law school, Mr. Wilinsky was a Financial Analyst in the Economic Research group at Goldman, Sachs & Co. A 1991 graduate of New York University School of Law, Mr. Wilinsky was a staff editor of the New York University Review of Law and Social Change, in which he published a note, Mending the Safety Net's Safety Net: The Federal Courts Study Committee's Proposals for Reforming the Social Security Disability Benefits Review Process, 18 N.Y.U. Rev. L. & Soc. Ch. 1079 (1990–1991). After graduating from law school, Mr. Wilinsky served as a law clerk to the Hon. Barbara A. Lee, United States Magistrate Judge, in the United States District Court for the Southern District of New York from 1991 to 1993. From 1993 to 1997, Mr. Wilinsky was associated with Leventhal & Slade, a federal litigation boutique.

Mr. Wilinsky concentrates in commercial, employment, and civil litigation and is admitted to practice in the State and Federal Courts of New York and New Jersey. Reported cases include Biancone v. Bossi, 806 N.Y.S.2d 694 (2d Dep't 2005); Hassan v. Bellmarc Prop. Mgmts. Svcs., Inc. 784 N.Y.S.2d 523 (1st Dep't 2004); Harlem Commonwealth Council, Inc. v. Thomas Memorial Wesleyan Methodist Church, 782 N.Y.S. 2d 83 (1st Dep't 2004); Kennedy v. Sprague, No. 02 Civ. 8590 (DLC), 2003 WL 43378 (S.D.N.Y. Jan. 7, 2003); and In re Crazy Eddie Securities Litigation, 948 F. Supp. 1154 (E.D.N.Y. 1996). In addition to commercial and civil litigation, Mr. Wilinsky concentrates in estate planning, trusts and estates administration and probate, as well as family law matters.

Mr. Wilinsky has been named a "Superlawyer." Mr. Wilinsky has also been awarded an AV rating for his professionalism and the quality of his legal work from Martindale-Hubbell, the premier directory of legal professionals. Additionally, Mr. Wilinsky was selected as a Top Rated Lawyer in Commercial Litigation by American Lawyer Media and Martindale Hubbell, as well as a Top Attorney in the New York Metropolitan Area. Mr. Wilinsky also received a "Best for Civil Litigation—New Jersey" from AI Global Media.

NOTES

Chapter One

1. Retrieved from https://www.therandomvibez.com/17-funny-monday -morning-quotes-deal-happily/.
2. Yujie Zhan, Mo Wang, Songqi Liu, and Kenneth S. Shultz, "Bridge Employment and Retirees' Health: A Longitudinal Investigation," *Journal of Occupational Health Psychology* 14, no. 4 (October 2009): 374–89.
3. Kevin Loria, "How Winning the Lottery Affects Happiness, According to Psychology Research," *Business Insider*, August 26, 2017. Retrieved from https://www.sciencealert.com/how-winning-the-lottery-affects-happiness -according-to-psychology-research.
4. https://news.gallup.com/poll/241649/employee-engagement-rise.aspx.
5. George C. Homans, *Social Behavior: Its Elementary Forms* (New York: Harcourt, Brace & World, 1961).

Chapter Two

1. Mark McLaughlin, *Cognitive Dominance: A Brain Surgeon's Quest to Out-Think Fear* (Egremont, MA: Black Irish Entertainment, LLC, 2019).
2. Oprah Winfrey, 2020 Vision: Your Life in Focus Tour, Charlotte, NC, January 18, 2020.
3. Winfrey, 2020 Vision.
4. J. Dispenza, *Becoming Supernatural: How Common People Are Doing the Uncommon* (Carlsbad, CA: Hay House, 2017).
5. Winfrey, 2020 Vision.
6. Dispenza, *Becoming Supernatural: How Common People Are Doing the Uncommon.*

7. Dispenza, *Becoming Supernatural: How Common People Are Doing the Uncommon.*

8. https://qz.com/835076/leonard-cohens-anthem-the-story-of-the-line-there-is-a-crack-in-everything-thats-how-the-light-gets-in/.

Chapter Three

1. J. L. Pierce, D. G. Gardner, L. L. Cummings, and R. B. Dunham, "Organizational Based Self-Esteem: Construct Definition Measurement and Validation," *Academy of Management Journal* 32 (1989):622–48.

2. Carol Dweck, *Mindset: The New Psychology of Success: How We Can Learn to Fulfill Our Potential* (New York: Ballantine Books, 2006).

3. David Rock, Beth Jones, and Chris Weller, "Using Neuroscience to Make Feedback Work and Feel Better," strategy+business, August 27, 2018, https://www.strategy-business.com/article/Using-Neuroscience-to-Make-Feedback-Work-and-Feel-Better?gko=9ff55.

4. P. Rozin and E. B. Royzman, "Negativity Bias, Negativity Dominance, and Contagion," *Personality and Social Psychology Review* 5, no. 4 (2001): 296–320.

5. J. D. Creswell, J. M. Dutcher, W. M. P. Klein, P. R. Harris, and J. M. Levine, "Self-Affirmation Improves Problem-Solving Under Stress," *PLoS ONE* 8, no. 5 (2013): e62593, https://doi.org/10.1371/journal.pone.0062593. D. K. Sherman and G. L. Cohen, "The Psychology of Self-Defense: Self-Affirmation Theory," *Advances in Experimental Social Psychology* 38 (2006): 183–242. D. K. Sherman, "Self-Affirmation: Understanding the Effects," *Social and Personality Psychology Compass* 7, no. 11 (November 2013): 834–45.

6. Elana Lyn Gross, "8 Managers Share the Best Way to Ask for a Raise (and Get It)," *Forbes*, June 27, 2016, https://www.forbes.com/sites/elanagross/2016/06/27/8-managers-share-the-best-way-to-ask-for-a-raise-and-get-it/#144329b374ff.

7. Society for Human Resource Management, retrieved from https://www.shrm.org/resourcesandtools/tools-and-samples/exreq/pages/details.aspx?erid=145.

Chapter Four

1. Marcus Buckingham, *Go Put Your Strengths to Work* (New York: Free Press, 2007).

2. Buckingham, *Go Put Your Strengths to Work.*

3. Buckingham, *Go Put Your Strengths to Work.*

4. Buckingham, *Go Put Your Strengths to Work.*

5. Mihaly Csikszentmihalyi, *Flow: The Psychology of Optimal Experience* (New York: Harper & Row, 1990).

6. Buckingham, *Go Put Your Strengths to Work.*
7. Buckingham, *Go Put Your Strengths to Work.*
8. Buckingham, *Go Put Your Strengths to Work.*

Chapter Six

1. M. D. Liberman and N. I. Eisenberger, "Pain and Pleasures of Social Life," *Science* 323, no. 5916 (February 13, 2009): 890–91.
2. Shawn Achor, *The Happiness Advantage: How a Positive Brain Fuels Success in Work and Life* (New York: Crown Business, 2010).
3. T. F. Heatherton, "Neuroscience of Self and Self-Regulation," *Annual Review of Psychology* 62 (2011): 363–90.
4. N. Eisenberger, "The Pain of Social Disconnection: Examining the Shared Neural Underpinnings of Physical and Social Pain," *Nature Reviews Neuroscience* 1 (2012): 421–34.
5. E. Gordon, *Integrative Neuroscience: Bringing Together Biological, Physiological and Clinical Models of the Human Brain* (Singapore: Harwood Academic Publishers, 2000).
6. D. Rock and C. Cox, *SCARF in 2012: Updating the Social Neuroscience of Collaborating with Others*, NeuroLeadership Institute, 2012.
7. Peter Senge, *The Fifth Discipline: The Art and Practice of the Learning Organization* (New York: Doubleday, 1990).

Chapter Seven

1. A. Wrzesniewski and J. Dutton, "Crafting a Job: Revisioning Employees as Active Crafters of Their Work," *Academy of Management Review* 26, no. 2 (2001): 179–201.
2. A. Wrzesniewski, C. McCauley, P. Rozin, and B. Schwartz, "Jobs, Careers, Callings: People's Relations to Their Work," *Journal of Research Personality* 31 (1997): 21–33.
3. Wrzesniewski et al., "Jobs, Careers, Callings."
4. Wrzesniewski et al., "Jobs, Careers, Callings."
5. Wrzesniewski et al., "Jobs, Careers, Callings."
6. J. Berg, A. Wrzesniewski, and J. Dutton, "Perceiving and Responding to Challenges in Job Crafting at Different Ranks: When Proactivity Requires Adaptivity," *Journal of Organizational Behavior* 31(2010): 158–86.
7. Berg, Wrzesniewski, and Dutton, "Perceiving and Responding to Challenges in Job Crafting."
8. Brené Brown, in her book *Rising Strong: How the Ability to Reset Transforms the Way We Live, Love, Parent, and Lead*, uses the phrase, "The story I'm making up." This is an adaption of her phrase. Thank you, Brené, for all the good you do in the world!

9. K. Patterson, J. Grenny, R. McMillan, and A. Switzler, *Crucial Conversations: Tools for Talking When Stakes Are High* (New York: McGraw-Hill, 2012).

Appendix C

1. Martin E. P. Seligman, *Flourish: A Visionary New Understanding of Happiness and Well-Being* (New York: Free Press, 2011).

ACKNOWLEDGMENTS

One of my writer friends warned me that the second book is harder than the first one. She was right! This book would not be in the world without the immense support, encouragement, and love of numerous people.

When I was stuck and in resistance and questioned my ability to write, AJ Harper, my writing coach, would lift me up, tell me truth, and send me back to work. She is an incredibly talented writer, storyteller, and coach. Thank you, AJ!

You are a rock star, Wendelyn Kelly! This book would not be possible without you! You skillfully, graciously, and compassionately manage all our clients, vendor partners, and team members. You kept the company and me on track when I would disappear into my creative zone for days and weeks. Thank you! It is my honor to work with you!

The creativity, graphic design, and marketing magic of Nancy Hala, Becca Levian, JC Lozano, and Ashleigh Respicio are extraordinary! Thank you for our brand, our marketing campaigns, and phenomenal ideas. And thank you to Sandy Smith and her entire team for her PR magic!

To Michelle Martin for believing in me and this book. Her relentless commitment to excellence and support of her clients is extraordinary. Thank you!

To Cheryl Segura, my talented editor, for her support, internal advocacy of my book, and commitment to its promise for the reader, and to the entire staff at McGraw Hill for your dedication and tireless support. Thank you.

To all my clients for lending me your stories and allowing me to serve you. Thank you!

Thank you to my early readers who provided invaluable feedback—Gail Angelo, Elizabeth Glontz, Bart Reed, Katie Trotter, and Angie Zimmern.

To Georgi Dienst, my soul sister who is always up for one of my wild adventures, who makes me laugh until tears run down my cheeks, and who also wondered what the green stuff was on the floor in India. To Sabrina Tully for being my wise teacher, coach, and "believing eyes." To Gail Angelo for her sage, soulful council. To Meghan Murphy for getting up before the sun to run and solve all the world's problems. And to the girls' night out crew for the laughs and the occasional headache. Love and hugs to all of you incredible women!

My daughter EC, you are a brilliant light in this world! You are kind, loving, wise beyond your years, my favorite traveling companion and deepest love. You keep me laughing, living in the precious present, and awake to my spirit.

Most important and with so much love, respect, and gratitude to my husband, Andrew. There were many days and weeks when you were the captain *and* cocaptain on the Tate ship. Thank you for your support, encouragement, and love. My current job is my dream job.

INDEX

COACHING.
WORKSHOPS.
CONSULTATIONS.

Want additional support to implement these tools and strategies?

Carson Tate and her team of coaches present and consult internationally with individuals, organizations, corporations, and small businesses, equipping them with tools, strategies, information, and insights that inspire employees and leaders to use their gifts and talents to achieve success.

To schedule a one-on-one consultation, coaching session, or private workshop with Carson Tate, visit www.carsontate.com.

To find an updated schedule of workshops and online courses, visit www.carsontate.com/learn.

ABOUT THE AUTHOR

CARSON TATE believes that work can be the full expression of who we are—the vehicle that takes us to a place where we reach the full potential of our greatness. As a visionary in the field of personal productivity and organizational excellence, Carson uses practical advice and empathetic training to guide and support her clients, helping them shine more brightly than they ever imagined possible.

An author, teacher, and coach, for 15 years Carson has worked with organizations of all sizes around the world to help them improve the engagement of their employees, the productivity of their workforces, and the efficacy of their leadership. It is her mission to change *how and why* we work so that we can each make a greater impact on our own lives, on our communities, and on the world at large.

Central to Carson's vision is her belief that when we do work that matters to us, it leads to greater success and wealth. It becomes the foundation of a harmonious life where we have the time, space, mental clarity, physical well-being, and emotional energy to take care of ourselves and others.

Carson Tate is also the founder of Working Simply, Inc., where she equips organizations with tools, strategies, information, and insights that inspire employees and leaders to use their gifts and talents to build their legacies.

Carson's signature courses include:

- Tame Your Inbox: How Email Can Work for You

- Work Well with Others: Find Joy in Teamwork

- Work Smarter, Not Harder: Get Up Close and Personal with Work

- The WORKshop: How to Work Simply and Live Fully

- Carson Tate Masterclass: Own It. Love It. Make It Work.

A prolific public speaker, Carson teaches audiences how to identify what success looks like from a personal and professional vantage point; how to move beyond the way we're working today, into a new world of productivity and accomplishment; and how to "own it, love it, make it work" by breathing life and inspiration into work.

Carson is a staunch advocate and champion for fair and flexible workplace practices that create healthy, nurturing environments for workers everywhere. Her goal is to shift the focus from output to impact—our value as workers is meant to be measured by our contribution.

There's nothing Carson loves more than connecting with people. In her uplifting and empowering courses, one-on-one coaching, speeches, and workshops, Carson shares surprising ideas and insights that clients and audiences can immediately apply to create fulfilling lives that align with their values and priorities. She inspires people to craft a future for themselves in which their work plays a joyful role. Above all, Carson believes that work is where your mission meets your spirit.

Contact Carson at www.carsontate.com.